WHAT GOD REALLY THINKS ABOUT WOMEN

SHARON JAYNES

HARVEST HOUSE PUBLISHERS

EUGENE, OREGON

Cover photo © iStockphoto / susabell

Cover by Garborg Design Works, Savage, Minnesota

WHAT GOD REALLY THINKS ABOUT WOMEN
Copyright © 2010 by Sharon Jaynes
Published by Harvest House Publishers
Eugene, Oregon 97402
www.harvesthousepublishers.com

Library of Congress Cataloging-in-Publication Data
    Jaynes, Sharon.
    What God really thinks about women / Sharon Jaynes.
        p. cm.
    ISBN 978-0-7369-2671-3 (pbk.)
    1. Women in the Bible. 2. Jesus Christ—Relations with women. 3. Bible. N.T. Gospels—
Criticism, interpretation, etc. 4. Christian women—Religious life. I. Title.
    BT590.W6J39 2010
    225.8'3054—dc22
                                                                                2009052971

Printed in the United States of America
               10 11 12 13 14 15 16 17 18 / BP-SK/ 10 9 8 7 6 5 4 3 2 1

This book is dedicated to the men and women of Campus Crusade for Christ who have worked so diligently to make the Magdalena project a reality. I pray that all who see the film, Magdalena: Through Her Eyes, will know just how much God loves and cherishes women.

Acknowledgments

Many men and women have influenced my life and challenged me to walk over to a fresh canvas and read the Gospels with new eyes:

Naomi Gingerich, who challenged me years ago to reconsider my own ideas about women in ministry.

Carolyn Custis James, who opened my eyes to God's unique design for His female image bearers as *ezers*, and who broadened my understanding of just what a *helper* was meant to be.

Campus Crusade, whose mission to reach out to women all around the world through the Magadalena project and subsequent film, *Magdalena: Through Her Eyes*. Specifically, Jenny Steinbach, Gail Ratzlaff, and Bill Sims, who caught the vision of how the Magdalena film and *What God Really Thinks About Women* manuscript could synergistically work to help women all around the world understand just how much God loves and cherishes His female image bearers.

My prayer team, who continually brings me before the Father.

My Girlfriends in God: Mary Southerland and Gwen Smith, who constantly cheer me on with encouraging words and lift me up with powerful prayer.

The Harvest House Publishers team: Bob Hawkins Jr., LaRae Weikert, Terry Glaspey, John Constance, and Barb Sherrill, who made the book possible; Shane White, Christianne Debysingh, and Abby Van Wormer, who made the book visible; Katie Lane, who made the book beautiful; and Betty Fletcher, who kept us all on schedule (no small feat). And my editor, Kim Moore, whose keen eye and kind heart made sure every word kept to the mission of helping women see themselves through Jesus' eyes.

My heavenly Father, who gently, tenderly, and sometimes sternly kept pointing me back to His Son, Jesus Christ, when I asked the hard questions regarding how He really felt about women.

Jesus Christ, who continually invited me to take a closer look at how He treated women against the backdrop of societal, political, and religious prejudices of His day.

The Holy Spirit, who confronted me, convicted me, and finally convinced me.

My husband, Steve, who daily holds up the mirror of God's Word for me to see myself as a dearly loved, cherished child of God, and encourages me to help other women see themselves as the same.

Contents

The Backdrop

The World
Jesus Stepped Into

She was beautiful.

She was bright.

And she was mad at God.

I sat across the lunch table picking at a salad and trying to digest Jan's words. Her startlingly teal eyes were tinted with frustration at God, primarily because of how she perceived He felt about women.

"I don't understand God. It seems like He is against women. He's set us up to fail. Even our bodies are weaker, and that just invites men to abuse us. All through the Bible I see how God used men in mighty ways. Abraham, Moses, David—you name it; it is always the men. And polygamy. How could God allow that? Today, there's so much abuse toward women. Where's God in all that? There are so many inequalities and injustices between how men are treated and how women are treated. What kind of God does that? I think the bottom line is that God just doesn't like women."

Jan knew her Bible. She grew up in church, had loving Christian parents, and accepted Christ when she was eight years old. "I accepted Jesus because I was afraid of hell," Jan confessed. "It wasn't because I had discovered a loving God who cared about me. I did it because of fear."

Regardless of why Jan became a Christian, her decision was real. She continued growing in her little-girl faith, and she even felt a call to ministry when she was in the eighth grade. She truly had a heart for the things of God.

But all during her growing up years, Jan felt she wasn't good enough. She saw herself as inferior to her younger brother, and she felt that her parents favored him over her. "They always paid more attention to my brother," she explained. "And if we got into a fight, my parents took up for him. 'Leave your brother alone,' they'd say. But I never heard, 'Leave your sister alone.'"

As is often the case with children, Jan's perception of her earthly father colored her perception of her heavenly Father, and the idea of male favoritism became the sieve through which her spiritual interpretations passed.

Jan graduated from high school with honors, from college with a degree in Communication Studies, and headed off to seminary. "When I got to seminary and started reading about some of the ancient philosophers' opinions of women, as well as some of the early church fathers, and even some modern day theologians, I just got mad. The more I read, the madder I got. Is it true? Are women less than men? Does God favor one gender over the other? As I considered my role as a woman in ministry, I couldn't find any role models."

Jan is now 26, a seminary graduate, and a secretary working in a growing church. She is frustrated, confused, and, as I mentioned earlier, just plain mad.

We talked for hours, and we have talked many more hours since then. Jan brought up some interesting questions. She was brave enough to voice what many women feel, and we struggled with her questions together. But I have done more than simply struggle with the difficult questions regarding God and how He views women. I have been on a 12-year journey to answer those tough questions for myself. God and I have spent many hours together as He opened my eyes to discover just what He really thinks about women. And I can't wait to share with you what I found.

For the most part, I was very happy in my ignorance and limited understanding of the roles and responsibilities of women in the body of Christ, but God wouldn't allow me to remain comfortable in my shallow understanding of His deep love and multifaceted plan for women. For far too long I had looked at women in the Bible through the wrong end of the telescope, making them appear far too small in comparison to their male counterparts. But God was needling me to be a good student and take a closer look. How thankful I am to the many men and women who have helped me grasp a clearer perspective of how God really feels about women.

For more than a decade I have studied, read, and prayed about women and their roles in the Bible. I have examined God's original intent at creation, the result of the fall, and Jesus' goal to set mankind free from the ravages of sin and the bondage of the enemy. I asked God how He really felt about women, and He showed me through the life of His Son.

When Philip asked Jesus to show him the Father, Jesus answered, "Anyone who has seen me has seen the Father" (John 14:9). The writer of Hebrews describes Jesus as "the exact representation of his [God's] being" (Hebrews 1:3). And while I don't presume to know the mind of God, I can understand His character and His ways through the ministry of Jesus, His Son.

Along this pilgrimage I was struck by Jesus' radical relationship with the women whose lives intersected with His during those 33 years He walked on this earth. He crossed man-made social, political, racial, and gender boundaries and addressed women with the respect due co-image bearers of God. But before we begin our journey of walking in these women's sandals, we need to grasp the darkened world into which Jesus stepped—the backdrop for God's redemptive plan for women to unfold.

In the Beginning...

When Jesus entered the world on that starry night in Bethlehem, His first cry echoed the heart cries of women who had been misused and abused for centuries. By the time Jesus took His first steps onto the dusty ground of Galilee, women were not allowed to talk to men in public, testify in court, or mingle with men at social gatherings. They were considered sensual temptresses and the chief cause of sexual sin. Women were considered a "lower animal species."[1] Men divorced their wives on a whim and tossed them out like burnt toast. Women lived in the shadows of society, and they were to be rarely seen and seldom heard. Much like a slave, a girl was the property of her father and later the property of her husband. Women were uneducated, unappreciated, and uncounted.

How did this happen? When and where did such a low regard of women begin? Certainly this was not God's intent.

It all began in the Garden of Eden.

If you have read any of my other books, you know I always like to start at the very beginning. So that's where we'll start today…in the beginning.

"In the beginning God created the heavens and the earth" (Genesis 1:1). Before the creation of the world, there was nothing. Then God spoke the world into existence. He said, "Let there be _____" and it was so (Genesis 1:3,6,9,14,20). God hung the sun and moon and then sprinkled stars about the expanse. He separated the dry ground from the seas and stocked both with vegetation and wildlife galore. Then, on the sixth day, God decided to do something extra special. "Let us make man in our own image, in our likeness, and let them rule over the fish of the sea and the birds of the air, over the livestock, over all the earth, and over all the creatures that move along the ground" (Genesis 1:26).

> The LORD God formed the man from the dust of the ground and breathed into his nostrils the breath of life, and the man became a living being (Genesis 2:7).

After each of the first five days of creation, as the sun set over the horizon, God said, "It is good." Six times, at the end of each phase of His handiwork, He reiterated His approval. We ride the rhythm of repetition only to be brought to a sudden halt by the Creator's words when He looked at the lone man with no suitable companion. "It is *not* good for the man to be alone" (Genesis 2:18).

And while God knew that it was not good for the man to be alone, He waited for Adam to come to the same conclusion.

> Now the LORD God had formed out of the ground all the beasts of the field and all the birds of the air. He brought them to the man to see what he would name them; and whatever the man called each living creature, that was its name. So the man gave names to all the livestock, the birds of the air and all the beasts of the field. But for Adam no suitable helper was found (Genesis 2:19-20).

Can't you just see Adam watching the animals prance and flit about, two by two, male and female? The bright red male cardinal and his demure grayish partner. The bushy-faced lion and his sleek, adoring lioness. The udder-dangling bovine and her fiery-eyed bull. Longingly, Adam observes the pairs of God's creation nuzzling, cuddling, and frolicking about. And while he was surrounded by noisy creatures and a loving God, Adam realized, in a sense, that he was all alone.

Adam's aloneness must have grown with each pair of animals that filed by to get their name tags. *What about me*, he might have mused as the last two creatures took flight. Oh, my friend, the best was yet to come!

> The LORD God caused the man to fall into a deep sleep; and while he was sleeping, he took one of the man's ribs and closed up the place with flesh. Then the LORD God made a woman from the rib he had taken out of the man (Genesis 2:21-22).

Bruce Marchiano paints a beautiful picture for us. "He shapes her frame and shades her skin. He molds her mind and measures her structure. He sculpts the contour of her face, the almonds of her eyes, and the graceful stretch of her limbs. Long before she has even spoken a word, he has held her voice in his heart, and so he ever so gently tunes its timbre. Cell by cell, tenderness by tenderness, and with care beyond care, in creation he quite simply loves her."[2]

When Adam woke from his God-induced anesthesia, he took one look at the fair Eve and I imagine he said, "Now *this* is good!" We don't know exactly what Adam's first words were when he initially laid eyes on Eve, but we do know his first recorded utterance appeared at her grand debut.

> This is now bone of my bones and flesh of my flesh; she shall be called woman, for she was taken out of man (Genesis 2:23).

What a beautiful portrait of Jesus' words, "Your Father knows what you need before you ask him" (Matthew 6:8). Yes, God knows what we need and often waits until we realize it before He provides. Had He created Adam and Eve simultaneously, Adam would have never known just how much he needed her.

Eve was the "crowning touch of God's creative masterpiece and the inspiration of man's first poetry."[3] She was not an afterthought, but God's grand finale. Woman was created to complete the picture of God's image bearer. Man could not do it alone. Woman could not do it alone. Both were necessary—working, serving, and living in tandem to complete the picture God intended all along.

God concluded the first week of the world's existence and the curtain fell with the words: "God saw all that he had made, and it was *very* good" (Genesis 1:31). With the debut of woman, what was "good" now became "very good."

God Created an Ezer

So who is this woman and why was she created? The Bible tells us she was created to be Adam's *helper.*

Like two pieces of a puzzle, Eve was created to complete man. "To complete" means "to fill up; that which is required to supply a deficiency; one or two mutually completing parts."

C.S. Lewis paints a beautiful picture:

> The Christian idea of marriage is based on Christ's words that a man and wife are to be regarded as a single organism—for that is what the words "one flesh" would be in modern English. And the Christians believe that when He said this He was not expressing a sentiment but stating a fact—just as one is stating a fact when one says that a lock and its key are one mechanism, or that a violin and a bow are one musical instrument. The inventor of the human machine was telling us that its two halves, the male and the female, were made to be combined together in pairs, not simply on the sexual level, but totally combined.[4]

Like a violin without a bow, or a lock without a key, man was incomplete without woman. Together, they were whole.

Let's look at Genesis 2:18 from several different translations of the Bible:

> The Lord God said, "It isn't good for man to be alone. I will make a companion for him, a *helper* suited to his needs" (TLB).

> The Lord God said, It is not good (sufficient, satisfactory) that man should be alone; I will make him a *helper* meet (suitable, adapted, complementary) for him (AMP).

> The LORD God said, "It is not good for the man to be alone. I will make a *helper* suitable for him" (NIV).

> The LORD God said, "It is not good that the man should be alone; I will make him a *helper* fit for him" (RSV).

> The LORD God said, "It is not good that the man should be alone; I will make him an *help* meet for him" (KJV).

While each translation of the Bible uses a different combination of words, they each have the word "helper" as a common thread ("help meet"—King James Version). It is the word "helper" that has caused much discussion and misunderstanding over the years, so let's address that right from the start. The Greek word for "helper" can also be translated "partner." Umberto Cassuto said, "Just as the rib is found at the side of the man and is attached to him, even so the good wife, the rib of her husband, stands at his side to be his helper-counterpart, and her soul is bound up with his."[5]

While some women may bristle at the thought of being called a mere "helper," we need only to look at the pages of Scripture to see that "helper" holds a place of great honor. The Hebrew word "helper" that is used for woman is *ezer*.[6] It is derived from the Hebrew word used of God and the Holy Spirit, "azar." Both mean "helper"—one who comes alongside to aid or assist. King David wrote, "O LORD, be my helper" (Psalm 30:10 NASB). "The LORD is with me; he is my helper" (Psalm 118:7). Moses said of God, "My father's God was my helper; he saved me from the sword of the Pharaoh" (Exodus 18:4).

Ezer appears twenty-one times in the Old Testament. Two times it is used of the woman in Genesis 2[7], sixteen times it is used of God or Yahweh as the helper of His people.[8] The remaining three references appear in the books of the prophets, who use it in reference to military aid.[9]

Theologian William Mounce explains:

> With so many references to God as our helper, it is obvious that an *ezer* is in no way inferior to the one who receives help. This is important because this is the word that God uses in Genesis 2:18 when he says about Adam, "It is not good for the man to be alone. I will make a *helper* suitable for him." God then forms Eve as his *ezer*. According to God's design, therefore, the man and the woman, the husband and the wife, have been designed by God to stand together and help each other fight the battles of life. And God is there as the divine *ezer* to fight with them.[10]

As Carolyn Custis James notes, "If language means anything, the *ezer*, in every case, is not a flunky or a junior assistant but a very strong helper."[11] Bible scholar Dr. Victor P. Hamilton explains:

The new creation (woman) will be neither a superior nor an inferior, but an equal. The creation of this helper will form one-half of a polarity, and will be to man as the south pole is the north pole...Any suggestion that this particular word denotes one who has only an associate or subordinate status to a senior member is refuted by the fact that most frequently this same word describes Yahweh's relationship to Israel. He is Israel's help(er).[12]

Whatever we may believe about a woman's roles in society and in the church, it is clear that man's aloneness was a dilemma that needed immediate attention. Woman is introduced as a partner in work, procreation, and companionship. Together they were to fill, subdue, and rule the earth. Together they shared a common calling. Yes, their roles and responsibilities may have been different. Our physical bodies would dictate such. But as far as being an image bearer of God to fill, subdue, and rule the earth, there was no distinction drawn at creation.

Strangely enough, Adam didn't need someone to do most of the tasks we usually associate with the role of the helper. His physical needs were abundantly met in the shelter and bounty of Eden. A wide variety of food was readily accessible in Eden, his well-stocked pantry. There were no menus to plan, groceries to buy, or meals to prepare. There was no house to decorate or floor to mop, table to set or children to nurture. There were no socks to pick up nor a stitch of laundry to clean. What is more, the first sewing project was a joint effort. Adam didn't wait behind a bush for Eve to sew fig leaves together for him. He did his own sewing. Hard to imagine that God would announce with fanfare a helper, who would do things that man could just as easily do for himself.[13]

Now, don't get me wrong. I love serving my husband and taking care of his needs. Strange as it may seem, I even enjoy cleaning the house! But those duties do not define the word *ezer*.

The beauty of the word *ezer* or "helper" is that God didn't define what that was to look like. He didn't write out male/female job descriptions or give Adam and Eve a list of prescribed duties. God said to both of them, "Be fruitful and increase in number; fill the earth and subdue it. Rule over the fish of the sea and the birds of the air and over every living creature that moves on the ground" (Genesis 1:28). Adam didn't say to Eve, "You take the birds and I'll take the fish." They ruled and subdued together.

There is nothing more beautiful than a husband and wife who have truly "become one flesh" and entered into the symbiotic dance of marriage, moving as one to the tune of God's love and the rhythm of His will—working together to be God's imagine bearers in the world.

But what about the woman who is not married? Is she an *ezer* as well? Absolutely. Woman was created to be a helper and rescuer no matter what her marital status in life. I was just as much God's warrior in the spiritual kingdom when I was single as I am today.

As I've already mentioned, the word *ezer* is used in the Old Testament two times in reference to woman as man's helper, sixteen times in reference to God as our Helper, and three times by the prophets in reference to military aid. However, each of the 16 times that the word is used for God, it also carries military connotations.

I was surprised to discover that even the Proverbs 31 woman, this woman who has been held up as a godly role model for centuries, was referred to in military terms. "An excellent wife, who can find?" the passage begins. "Her worth is far above jewels" (Proverbs 31:10 NASB). The New International Version calls her "a wife of noble character." The Amplified Bible describes her as "a capable, intelligent, and virtuous woman." The Hebrew word that is translated "excellent" or "virtuous" can also mean "wealthy, prosperous, valiant, boldly courageous, powerful, mighty warrior."

Did you catch that? "Mighty warrior." But before you suggest that we exchange our jeans for battle fatigues, brooms for rifles, and summer camps for boot camps, consider the words Paul wrote to

the churches in Ephesus and Corinth that encourage us to stand in
the spiritual battle as praying women armed with God's Word:

> Finally, be strong in the Lord and in his mighty power. Put
> on the full armor of God so that you can take your stand
> against the devil's schemes. For our struggle is not against
> flesh and blood, but against the rulers, against the author-
> ities, against the powers of this dark world and against the
> spiritual forces of evil in the heavenly realms (Ephesians
> 6:10-12).

> Though we live in the world, we do not wage war as the
> world does. The weapons we fight with are not the weap-
> ons of the world. On the contrary, they have divine power
> to demolish strongholds. We demolish arguments and
> every pretension that sets itself up against the knowledge
> of God, and we take captive every thought to make it obe-
> dient to Christ (2 Corinthians 10:3-5).

God didn't create woman simply because man was lonely, even
though that was obviously the case. He created woman to complete
man—to love with him, work with him, rule with him, live life
with him, procreate with him, and to fight alongside him. She was a
female image bearer in this mysterious union of marriage. Woman
was and is a warrior called to fight alongside man in the greatest battle that was yet to come—a battle not fought on the battlefield with
guns, but on our knees in prayer.

Why have I gone into such great length about this word *ezer*?
Because, dear friend, I want you to grasp the full impact of what
God created you to be. You are an amazing masterpiece of Almighty
creative genius. You are a woman.

After the Fall

So what happened? How did woman move from a mutual place
of honor as an image bearer in the Garden of Eden to the oppression we have seen through the centuries? Well, let's don't leave the
garden quite yet.

Chapter 3 of Genesis begins with these daunting words: "Now the serpent…" Satan was not happy about these image bearers God had created. Even though he had once been an angel of light, Satan had been cast to the earth with one-third of the angels because of their rebellion against God (Revelation 12:4). He knew he was doomed and wanted to take as many of God's image bearers with him as possible. So he started with the first two.

We don't have clear evidence as to why Satan engaged Eve in conversation regarding eating the forbidden fruit, but we do know that Adam stood passively by as the drama unfolded. Even though Genesis 3 states that Satan addressed "the woman," he used the Hebrew plural form of "you" when he spoke. He wasn't just talking to her.

Some say that the sin began when Eve tried to get the upper hand in the relationship, but there was no upper hand to get. Adam and Eve lived in harmony with each other. They moved as one. If she had been trying to get the upper hand, then she would have kept the fruit to herself and not offered it to her husband as well.

Some say that Adam sinned because he listened to his wife. But Eve wasn't created to be a silent partner. It wasn't that he listened to her as a woman, but that he listened to what she said and ate the fruit.[14]

In the end, both Adam and Eve disobeyed God, believed Satan's lie, and suffered the consequences of a broken relationship with God and spiritual death. We, dear friends, suffer the consequences even today. At that moment of disobedience, fear and shame entered the world and the first man and the first woman tried to hide from God.

"Where are you," God called as He uttered the first question recorded in the Bible (Genesis 3:9). That is the question He still asks today as He longs to have a restored relationship with His image bearers. "Where are you?" God brought Adam and Eve out in the open, confronted their sin, and explained the consequences to come.

The serpent, the woman, and the man were all judged, but only the serpent and the ground were cursed. God's judgment on the serpent foreshadowed events that were yet to come—the day Jesus Christ would crush Satan's head with His heel. Satan clearly understood that his demise would come from a woman's womb. And from the very beginning, Satan has been decked out in full battle array to destroy her.

Another result of the fall was that man would rule over the woman. When Adam spoke to God about their sin, he said, "The woman you put here *with* me" (Genesis 3:12). Previously, they ruled together, but all that was about to change. "Your desire will be for your husband," God explained to Eve. "And he will rule over you" (verse 16). From that time on, relational tension between man and woman was the norm.

But the good news for us is that God loves turning things around. While the tree in the garden brought death and the curse, the tree of Calvary brought life and blessing. Jesus came to set the captive free. He came to destroy the works of the devil (1 John 3:8). But thousands of years were sandwiched between God's words about Jesus, "He will," and our Savior's words, "I have." And, unfortunately, women have been devalued, defiled, and degraded in every way imaginable.

Between the Garden of Eden and the Garden of Gethsemane

Many years passed before God's kingdom calendar signaled that Jesus' redemptive plan was to begin. In order to grasp just how radically liberating Jesus' actions and teaching were for women, we need to understand the world Jesus stepped into.

Much of the ancient world was influenced by philosophers and their teachings. For most of us, ancient philosophy is far removed and of little interest. However, in the fifth century BC, it affected the entire culture. It was the philosophers' teaching and influence that shackled women and kept them in bondage to a patriarchal society.

For example, in ancient Athens, a city named after the beautiful goddess of wisdom, philosophers held to the belief that women were inferior to men on every level. These philosophers created the lens through which much of the civilized world looked at life. Socrates (470–399 BC) argued that being born a woman was a divine punishment, since a woman is halfway between a man and an animal.[15] Respectable Greek wives led secluded lives and rarely appeared in social situations. They took no part in public affairs and rarely appeared at meals or social occasions to mingle with the men.[16]

Socrates taught Plato, who then passed his teaching along to Aristotle. Plato believed that women were a "degenerate form of manly perfection," and that men who did not live righteous lives would be reincarnated as females.[17] He believed that this is how the entire female gender came into existence.[18]

Aristotle declared, "The courage of a man is shown in commanding, of a woman in obeying."[19] He taught that women were inferior and needed to be commanded by men and used for their pleasure. Men serious about their studies were encouraged to avoid women altogether, as women were considered a distraction and temptation.

Demosthenes, who was a noted orator during Aristotle's day, stated that the role of Athenian woman was as follows: "We have courtesans for our pleasures, prostitutes [that is, young female slaves] for daily physical use, wives to bring up legitimate children and to be faithful stewards in household matters."[20]

Aristotle left the world with a collection of fascinating studies on a variety of subjects. He observed the nature of bees and noted how the swarm was led by one apparent leader, which he assumed was the "king bee." It would be centuries later before naturalists would discover the leader was indeed a "queen bee."[21] (You go, girl.)

Young girls were married at a very early age and received no education except on how to run a household. They never went out of the home alone, shared a public meal with men, or entered into community life. Women were not only considered inferior, but also a distraction and danger to men who desired to pursue wisdom.

The ancients believed that life came from a man's semen, where tiny human beings were stored. Women simply served as the soil in which the seed was planted and allowed to grow until birth. They knew nothing of a woman's eggs and therefore drew conclusions from only what their naked eyes could see (no pun intended). It wasn't until the 1800s that scientists discovered a woman had eggs. Before that she was considered just a holding tank. It makes sense that if women are thought of as "dirt," they will be treated like dirt.

The Romans didn't view women quite as harshly as the Greeks, but they still believed that women needed to be kept under a man's control.[22] The Romans were more progressive as to what activities a woman could engage in outside the home, but her reach wasn't far from her front door. If a woman was caught in adultery, Roman law gave the husband the right to kill her because she was his property. However, a man could have sexual relations outside of marriage at will.[23] Roman men tended to share the Greek view of women as objects of pleasure or else sources of temptation.[24]

These philosophers were bright men who were obviously deceived by the enemy himself. "There is nothing so foolish as an intelligent man using his mental gifts to explain away the simplicity of the truth."[25] It would be very easy to raise our ire against the philosophers of the past, or even those in Middle Eastern countries who continue to treat women with the same disdain today, but I always go back to the source. It is the devil himself who has the destruction of women in his game plan.

In the Jewish culture, women were not treated much better than their Roman and Greek sisters. Even though the Old Testament is filled with influential women—such as Deborah the prophetess, who advised military leaders; Esther the queen, who saved the Jews from annihilation; Rahab the harlot, who rescued the spies from soldiers of Jericho; Abigail the farmer's wife, who stopped King David's needless assassination plan, just to name a few—women were still considered a commodity.

The Jewish people became more integrated with and influenced by foreign cultures that oppressed women. By the time Jesus was born, women were not allowed to talk to a man in public...even to their husbands. If a woman spoke to a man in public who was not her husband, it was assumed she was having a relationship with him and grounds for divorce. Women were not allowed to eat in the same room with a gathering of men, to be educated in the Torah (the Scriptures) with men, or to enter the inner court of the temple to worship with men. Two thousand years ago, Rabbi Eliezer stated, "Rather should the words of the Torah be burned than entrusted to a woman!"[26]

A rabbi might not even speak to his own daughter or sister in public. Some Pharisees were referred to as "the bruised and bleeding ones" because they would shut their eyes whenever they saw a woman on the street, and therefore they often walked into walls and houses.[27] Each morning a Pharisee began his day by thanking God that He had not made him a "Gentile, a woman, or a slave."[28]

A woman was considered the property of her father. That ownership was passed to her husband when she married and to her son when she was widowed. There was little hope for a woman devoid of all three. She was not allowed to go out in public without a suitable male escort. This was "not so much to protect her, but to protect her husband's name from any slips she might make…through improper conduct. Any males who wished to address her had to do so through her chaperone, not directly."[29]

A woman was not considered a credible witness and was not allowed to testify in court. Feminine voices and flowing hair were considered sensual and seen as a temptation to men. Women were considered the dregs of society and were thought responsible for much of the evil in the world. They were segregated in the social and religious life of their communities and considered to be inferior, unteachable creatures whose sole purpose was domesticity and sexual pleasure.[30]

I could say more, but I think this is enough to allow us to catch a glimpse of how women were viewed and why. It was ugly. It was dark. It was oppressive. That is the world Jesus stepped into. That is the backdrop for God's ultimate drama of redemption to unfold.

Why did Jesus come to earth? John tells us in a nutshell. "The reason the Son of God appeared was to destroy the devil's work" (1 John 3:8). Jesus came to restore God's original design and purpose for men and women that was distorted and disturbed in the garden. He came to restore fallen humanity in every sense of the word. Part of that restoration included restoring Eve to her position she enjoyed before the fall. Jesus walked on the scene to see God's female image bearers hidden in the shadows behind lock and key, and He flung the doors open wide.

It is easy for us of the twenty-first century to view Jesus' interaction with women as somewhat ordinary, but then it was radical in every sense of the word. Jesus was so far out on a limb, it was a good thing He made the tree. When we understand a bit of the Roman and Greek philosophy and treatment of women at the time Jesus appeared on the earth, we can better understand just how radical Jesus' treatment of women really was. He took these devalued and degraded female image bearers and placed them center stage to play leading roles in God's redemptive plan.

Simply put—Jesus shook the house.

A New Day for Women

As we turn the page from Malachi 4:6 to Matthew 1:1, as God breaks 400 years of silence, we get a hint that a new day is on the horizon. In the Old Testament genealogies, families were traced through the males only. However, in the genealogy of Jesus Christ, four women are listed along with Mary: Tamar, Rahab, Ruth, and Bathsheba. The very fact that women were mentioned at all is reason for pause.

The rhythm of "the father of, the father of, the father of," comes to a screeching halt as a woman's name appears on the page. "... Zerah, whose mother was Tamar" (Matthew 1:3). Then the usual cadence picks right back up where it left off with "the father of, the father of, the father of." Once again, the harmonious flow is abruptly arrested with "Boaz, whose mother was Rahab, Boaz the father of Obed, whose mother was Ruth" (Matthew 1:5).

Friend, the fact that a woman's name was even mentioned in the genealogy gives us a big hint that something is different. God is up to something new. It's time for the female image bearers to come out of the shadows and into the light. How exciting that that light is the light of Christ. Jesus welcomed women into His company, included them in His parables, and invited them to be a part of His ministry team.

The focus of this book is to discover what God really thinks about women. That sounds a bit presumptuous, doesn't it? The prophet Isaiah wrote, "Who has understood the mind of the LORD or instructed him as his counselor?" (Isaiah 40:13). This same verse is repeated by Paul in Romans 11:34 and 1 Corinthians 2:16. At the same time, our greatest joy in life is found in knowing God.

J.I. Packer, in his modern classic *Knowing God,* points out:

> The world becomes a strange, mad, painful place, and life in it a disappointing and unpleasant business for those who do not know about God. Disregard the study of God, and you sentence yourself to stumble and blunder through life blindfolded, as it were, with no sense of direction and no understanding of what surrounds you.[31]

So how do we know God? Can we really understand what He thinks about any subject? Certainly the mind of God is a fathomless sea of wisdom that our finite minds will never totally comprehend, but at the same time He longs for us to know Him. God created us to be in relationship with Him, and as in all intimate relationships, a deep understanding exists between both parties. Of course, God knows us totally and completely. And, amazingly, He invites us to be in relationship with Him and know Him as well. Whether it is understanding what God thinks about marriage or money, sin or salvation, worry or worship, the answers are in the Bible for us to discover.

Paul wrote to the Corinthians that "the man who thinks he knows something does not yet know as he ought to know" (1 Corinthians 8:2). In other words, no matter how much we may know about God, a wise woman understands that she knows very little. But with that reality, we still strike out to unearth the treasures hidden in knowing God.

In His infinite wisdom, God has given us many ways to learn of His character and His ways. We learn of Him through His Word, through creation, and most of all through His Son. Jesus, in one of His final conversations with the disciples, explained: "If you really knew me, you would know my Father as well...Anyone who has seen me has seen the Father" (John 14:7,9).

Eugene Peterson, in his paraphrase, *The Message*, says it this way: "To see me is to see the Father...The words that I speak to you aren't mere words. I don't just make them up on my own. The Father who resides in me crafts each word into a divine act" (John 14:9).

Jesus spoke exactly what the Father told Him to speak[32] and did exactly what His Father told him to do.[33] He was the "image of the invisible God,"[34] and "the exact representation of his being."[35]

So can we really know what God thinks? To some extent, the answer is yes. We only have to look at the life and ministry of His Son.

The focus of this book is JESUS and how He called women out of the shadows of society and placed them center stage. It is about how He came to liberate and set women free—a freedom that has not been duplicated in any other world religion. What do I mean by "set women free"? There are two aspects of this freedom that we will explore.

Jesus came to set women free from...

Jesus came to set women free to...

He did not set women free only to be quarantined in the new order called the church. He set women free to go out into the world to tell the Good News of the gospel and to work among believers to build the body of Christ. In a culture that kept women tucked away in the recesses of the home to be neither seen nor heard, Jesus pulls them from behind the scenes, positions them front and center, and shines on them the spotlight of His divine love and calling. As the curtain of the New Testament rises, women fill the stage and take starring roles as God's grand drama of redemption unfolds.

Jesus made deliberate choices in the *who, what, when,* and *where* of His teachings and miracles. It was no accident that many of His healings occurred on the Sabbath. It was no accident that many of His conversations were with women. It was no accident that women were the recipients of many of His miraculous healings. It was no accident that the "least of these" received the best of Him.

Jesus took the keys of truth and unlocked the shackles to liberate women from the oppression that had them bound and sequestered in the nooks and crannies of society. How proud I am of those women who accepted Jesus' invitation to come out of hiding. They were agents who listened to the call of God above the oppressive voices of the culture.

In our time together, we are going to visit with the women in Jesus' life and ministry. When we read the Gospels with such familiarity we may miss the wonder and awe of Jesus' radical, life-changing words. We tend to run His words through a sieve of cultural norms and childhood teachings rather than lay them on a fresh canvas. The words become muddied and muted when they are splashed on old landscapes of cracked hues.

Let's walk over to a new easel. One on which an untouched canvas awaits. In the tray lie Jesus' words—new, fresh, vibrant, and alive. We'll not paint them on the old canvas of our minds, hoping to cover up the misinterpreted words that have gone before. We'll look at them with fresh eyes.

Let's get to know a few of the women who encountered the Liberator and began a new life of freedom. Come with me and sit by the well with the Samaritan woman expecting insult and rejection, but receiving acceptance and love. Stand with the woman caught in adultery expecting condemnation and death, but finding forgiveness and a chance to start anew. Reach with the bleeding woman to touch the hem of His garment in secret, only to be healed and publically affirmed. Rise from the ruins of life with Mary Magdalene, and run with purpose to announce the miracle of Jesus' resurrection. As we encounter each woman Jesus impacts, I pray you will write your name into the script and experience Him as never before.

Let's observe how Jesus treated God's female image bearers to discover what God really thinks about women.

THE LEADING LADIES

2

JUST AN ORDINARY GIRL
(MARY OF NAZARETH)

Freed from an Ordinary Life
Freed to Fulfill an Extraordinary Purpose

Traveling down the dusty road to Bethlehem on the lumpy backbone of a donkey was hard enough, but being jostled along while nine-months pregnant was an arduous task accompanied by troublesome shoots of pain. The two blankets Joseph had placed over the hairy beast did little to cushion the jarring rough ride for his young bride and mother-to-be.

"How are you faring?" a concerned Joseph asked.

"I just hope this baby is more comfortable than I am," Mary breathed. "I don't think He's going to wait much longer to make His grand debut."

Mary smiled as she thought about the child nestled in her womb. *Who would have ever thought the Savior of the world would spend His last few moments before entering the world riding on the back of a donkey? Who would have ever thought the Messiah would be born to such as me?*

Mary's thoughts went back to the day the angel Gabriel appeared to her and announced God's redemptive plan.

"Mary," her mother called. "Are you finished kneading the dough?

Don't forget to milk the goat. And then there's the robe that is half finished. It seems our work is never done!"

At 15, Mary had a full schedule of daily activities simply keeping the home running smoothly. But soon enough it would no longer be her father's house she served, but her husband's. The marriage between her and Joseph had been arranged since she was a child, but that did not diminish romantic notions of being swept away in the middle of the night by her handsome groom. Their engagement was a legally binding contract, and all that remained were the technicalities—the actual wedding celebration.

If all goes well, I will be married to Joseph within a year's time. But then, what could go wrong? The contract has been signed, the bride price has been paid, and the room connected to his father's house is almost complete.

As the young maiden continued daydreaming about her new life to come, a golden presence filled the room. The hair on the back of her neck bristled as a gentle breeze brushed past her cheek. The window remained fastened while an indescribable stirring swirled around her. Looking up from her work, she was startled by the glowing figure standing before her.

A single gasp filled her lungs as Mary clasped her hand over her mouth. Wide eyes tried to make sense of the vision before her. Was it a man? A ghost? An angel? Was she dreaming?

"Greetings, highly favored one! The Lord is with you."

Seeing her pale before him, the angel Gabriel continued, "Do not be afraid, Mary. You have found favor with God. It is His plan that you will be with child and will give birth to a son, and you shall name Him Jesus. He will be great and will be called the Son of the Most High. God will give Him the throne of His father David, and He will reign over the house of Jacob forever. His kingdom will never end."

Mary's fear did not subside with this confusing proclamation, yet there was something comforting in the tone of this being's voice. While her soul began a calm descent, her mind began to race ahead.

A son? Pregnant? Jesus? Son of the Most High? A jumble of thoughts spilled out all at once as she tried to piece together the information lying like scattered puzzle pieces before her.

"How can this be? I am still a virgin."

Gabriel leaned in and held Mary's gaze. "The power of the Most High, through the Holy Spirit, will make this happen. The holy One you will bear will be called the Son of God."

Sensing her bewildered and troubled heart, the messenger knew she needed a bit more assurance. Perhaps she needed a friend. He leaned back and remarked, "Also, your relative Elizabeth is going to have a child in her old age. She who was said to be barren is already in her sixth month. Nothing is impossible with God."

With that reminder of God's omnipotent power, Mary embraced her calling. "May it be to me as you have said."

Then, just as quickly and quietly as he had appeared, the angel was gone.

Mary stood alone in the room trying to take in all that had happened. Questions buzzed in her mind like a swarm of bees. "I've got to get to Elizabeth," Mary whispered.

Right away, Mary packed her things and began her 60-mile journey from Nazareth to Judea. After several days, she arrived.

As soon as Mary entered the room, Elizabeth was filled with the Holy Spirit and began prophesying. In a loud voice she proclaimed: "Blessed are you among women, and blessed is the child you will bear! But why am I so favored, that the mother of my Lord should come to me? As soon as the sound of your greeting reached my ears, the baby in my womb leaped for joy. Blessed is she who has believed that what the Lord has said to her will be accomplished!"

A Closer Look

What an amazing encounter for one so young. God's plan of redemption was held by the thread of a teenage girl from Nazareth. Who knew it would be so strong?

We don't know exactly how old Mary was at the time of Gabriel's proclamation. Commentaries have suggested anywhere between 13 and 16—marrying age during those days.

Nazareth was considered an insignificant town, yet God used it in a significant way. Likewise, Mary was a seemingly insignificant girl, yet God chose her for a significant role in the most important story of all time. Her selfless surrender serves as an example of the impact obedience to God's call can have on our lives and on the lives of others as well.

So many questions come to mind. Let's start at the beginning and take a closer look.

Greetings, you who are highly favored! (Luke 1:28).

Just after Adam and Eve sinned and ate the forbidden fruit, God announced that the offspring of a woman would eventually crush the serpent's head (Satan) (Genesis 3:15). All along, it was God's redemptive plan for the Savior of the world to be born of a woman. God certainly didn't have to do it that way, but He chose to use a woman in the unfolding of salvation's plan.

But why Mary? Why that particular girl? What was it about her that caused God to choose her? We will never know the answers to those questions, but we can get a glimpse into God's heart by looking closely at the word "favored."

Gabriel greeted Mary by saying she was "highly favored." When we look at the word "favored," we realize that the choice had little to do with Mary and everything to do with God. The word "favor" is the Greek word *charis,* which is where we get the word "grace." Grace is unmerited, undeserved, unearned favor from God. It is a gift we don't earn or deserve, but are given simply because God wants to give it.

The Bible says that we are chosen by grace (Romans 11:5-6), saved by grace (Romans 3:24), and given spiritual gifts by grace (Romans 12:6). Paul says that God lavishes His grace on us (Ephesians 1:7-8). Don't you just love that? He doesn't dole out a teaspoon here and there, but He pours out His favor on us—He bathes us in His grace.

Why was Mary chosen? The same reason you and I were chosen to be His children. Because of His grace. We are not saved because we deserve it. She was not chosen because she deserved it. She was chosen because God's grace was with her.

The Lord is with you (Luke 1:28).

For many years I began each day praying for my son, "God, please be with Steven today." Then one day God stopped me mid-prayer. *Sharon, I am with Steven every day,* He seemed to say. *Why do you continue asking for something Steven already has?*

God was right! (Imagine that.) God was with Steven at all times, just as He is with you and me. He promised each of His children, "Never will I leave you; never will I forsake you" (Hebrews 13:5). After God's gentle nudge, I changed my prayer for Steven. "God, I pray that Steven will sense Your presence in his life today. Thank You for being with him."

Mary needed that same reassurance. The reminder of God's presence in her life would be crucial for the news that Gabriel was about to deliver.

> *Mary was greatly troubled at his words and wondered what kind of greeting this might be. But the angel said to her, "Do not be afraid, Mary, you have found favor with God. You will be with child and give birth to a son, and you are to give him the name Jesus. He will be great and be called the Son of the Most High. The Lord God will give him the throne of his father David, and he will reign over the house of Jacob forever; his kingdom will never end" (Luke 1:29-33).*

If Gabriel showed up at my door, I think "Do not be afraid" would be an appropriate greeting. As a matter of fact, it seems as though these are some of the first words God and His messengers spoke to many called on for special assignment. "Do not be afraid," God said to Abram (Genesis 15:1). "Do not be afraid," God said to Joshua (Joshua 8:1). "Do not be afraid," the angel said to Zechariah

(Luke 1:13). "Do not be afraid," the angel said to the shepherds (Luke 2:10).

And now, when God is calling an ordinary girl out of the shadows to stand center stage, He reassures her with the same courage-bolstering words that have echoed through the ages. "Do not be afraid...God is with you." And if anyone was going to need reassurance of God's presence in her life, it was Mary.

Gabriel then proceeded to tell her about her God-ordained assignment. She would conceive a Son by the power of the Holy Spirit and give Him the name Jesus. "Jesus" is the Greek form of the name Joshua, which means "the Lord saves." Mary was part of this fallen world, and like all of mankind, she needed a Savior. When Paul wrote, "All have sinned and fall short of the glory of God" (Romans 3:23)—that included Mary.

In Mary's own song of praise, she cried out, "My soul glorifies the Lord and my spirit rejoices in God my Savior" (Luke 1:46-47). Regardless of what artists have painted through the centuries, Mary did not have a halo over her head. She was a sinner, just like you and me. She was chosen because of God's grace, just like you and me. She was just an ordinary girl with an extraordinary calling.

God set the stage and called His first leading lady to take her position front and center. Who would have ever imagined she would take her place with such courage.

> *"How will this be," Mary asked the angel, "since I am a virgin?" (Luke 1:34).*

Mary's question didn't mean she doubted what the angel said was true. She simply questioned the logistics and sought clarity and direction. Her wonderment did not mean she was reluctant. She was just confused about the physiology of the process. She had never slept with a man, so how was this possible?

> *The angel answered, "The Holy Spirit will come upon you, and the power of the Most High will overshadow you. So*

*the holy one to be born will be called the Son of God. Even
Elizabeth your relative is going to have a child in her old age,
and she who was said to be barren is in her sixth month. For
nothing is impossible with God" (Luke 1:35-37).*

The angel saw the purity of her heart and went on to explain
exactly how this would occur. In a day when women were not for-
mally taught the Scriptures, Mary had a front row seat with one of
God's personal messengers for private tutoring.

We can savor the fact that Mary was one of Jesus' first disciples.
She was taught theology. She believed by faith. She obeyed by choice.

This heavenly decision caused an earthly dilemma. An unwed
pregnancy could lead to her parents disowning her, her fiancé
divorcing her, and her accusers stoning her to death. She had to
know she was called. God sent an angel to explain her calling and
sent her to Elizabeth for confirmation.

*"I am the Lord's servant," Mary answered. "May it be to me
as you have said" (Luke 1:38).*

When God called Moses to lead the Israelites out of Egyptian
captivity, Moses tried to convince Him to send someone else (Exodus 4:13). When God called Gideon to lead the Israelites into battle, Gideon reminded Him of his lack of credentials and asked for a
sign (Judges 6:17). When God called Jeremiah to be the next great
prophet, Jeremiah argued that he was far too young for the job (Jeremiah 1:6). When God appointed Jonah to preach repentance to the
people of Nineveh, he hopped on the next boat out of town (Jonah
1:3). But when God called Mary to bear His only Son, she accepted
the assignment with beauty and grace. "I am the Lord's servant,"
Mary answered. "May it be to me as you have said."

In Eugene Peterson's paraphrase, *The Message,* Mary said, "Yes, I see
it all now: I'm the Lord's maid, ready to serve. Let it be with me just as
you say." Another translation puts it this way: "Behold, the *bondslave*
of the Lord; may it be done to me according to your word" (NASB).

The Greek word for "bondslave" is *doulos* or *doule* (feminine form) and means "one who gives himself up to the will of another, without any idea of bondage."[1] In the Old Testament, "bondslave" referred to a slave set free who *chose* to stay with his master for the rest of his life. In the New Testament, the term was used figuratively of a Christian set free from the slavery of sin who *chose* to serve his Master, Jesus, for the rest of his life.

> *At that time Mary got ready and hurried to a town in the hill country of Judea, where she entered Zechariah's home and greeted Elizabeth. When Elizabeth heard Mary's greeting, the baby leaped in her womb, and Elizabeth was filled with the Holy Spirit. In a loud voice she exclaimed: "Blessed are you among women and blessed is the child you will bear! But why am I so favored, that the mother of my Lord should come to me? As soon as the sound of your greeting reached my ears, the baby in my womb leaped for joy" (Luke 1:39-44).*

Elizabeth is not one of the women we are focusing on in the pages of this book, but I cannot leave this chapter without shining the spotlight on this amazing prophet for just a moment. At God's prompting, Elizabeth met Mary on the stage, grabbed her by the hand, and joined her on the journey to fulfill an extraordinary purpose. But this was not simply a supporting role. She was a leading lady in her own right.

Elizabeth was more than an incubator for the forerunner of Jesus, John the Baptist. She was a prophet chosen by God to mentor the mother of His child. Elizabeth's grasp of the situation was remarkable! She understood that the baby Mary was carrying was the Messiah when even those closest to Jesus in future years would not. And why was that? It is simple, really. It was not because Elizabeth was especially smart. It is because the illuminating power of the Holy Spirit revealed it to her. And that is the same with you and me. We only understand spiritual truth when the Holy Spirit opens our eyes to see.

Isn't it wonderful that God created women for relationship? He knew that Mary was going to need a friend—a girlfriend. God is always with us, but sometimes He gives us like-minded friends with whom to walk the journey. It was a new day for women, and it all began with two cousins.

> *Blessed is she who has believed that what the Lord has said to her will be accomplished! (Luke 1:45).*

After Elizabeth's prophecy, Mary's thoughts burst forth in a flowing fountain of praise. Words from Scripture mingled with words from her own heart and spilled forth in a beautiful song. And while she sang with joy, this heavenly purpose would eventually cause earthly pain, as Simeon would warn in the days ahead.

Mary believed. Elizabeth said it well, "Blessed is she who has believed that what the Lord has said to her will be accomplished!" Could that be said of you? Could that be said of me? Do you believe God? Do you believe that what He has said He will accomplish? If so, then you, my friend, will experience the abundant life that God has planned all along. God is looking for a woman just like you! One who believes He is who He says He is, and believes He will do what He said He will do. Paul tells us that there is "incomparably great power for us who believe" (Ephesians 1:19).

As I mentioned before, the redemptive plan of God hung by the thread of a young Jewish girl. Mary risked everything: her reputation, her marriage, her family, her income, her dreams, and her life. She was an *ezer* who stepped out onto the battlefield, armed with faith in the One who called her. In doing so, she experienced breathtaking privilege accompanied by unspeakable pain.

Do you want to be a woman entrusted with God-sized assignments? Then memorize those words of Mary. May her words be our response to God each and every day of our lives: "I am the Lord's servant. May it be to me as you have said." No wonder God allowed Mary to participate in Jesus' earthly ministry and ignite the fuse that would change the world. Let's join her some 30 years later and discover just what happened.

Celebrating at the Wedding at Cana

It was a beautiful day for a wedding. Mary only hoped the good weather would hold out for the seven days of celebration that would follow. She was glad for the break in the mundane activities of running a household and looked forward to spending extended time with her Son.

"I hope you don't mind if I bring along a few friends," Jesus asked as He walked in from His work in the carpentry shop.

"Absolutely not. As long as they will behave and not embarrass the family," she teased.

Jesus turned to Mary with a look that pierced her soul. "These men have been chosen as well."

Chosen. There was that word again. And the feeling of normalcy began to slip through her fingers like grains of sand.

Jesus had grown strong and tall over the past 30 years. While Mary had seen glimpses of His divine nature, she continued to hold her breath for the day the angel prophesied would come to fruition. The words "Son of the Most High" and "his kingdom will never end" were never far from her memory. She recalled the stories of Jesus' baptism. God said, "This is my Son, whom I love; with him I am well pleased" (Matthew 3:17). Mary clung to the days of normalcy as long as she could, but she felt they were drawing to a close.

The bride was radiant and the groom proud as a freshly preened peacock. The wedding party and guests alike enjoyed a bountiful buffet, delightful dancing, and ambrosial wine. Gaiety and merriment filled the rooms with laughter and joyous chatter. There was nothing like a wedding party to wash away the doldrums of everyday life.

Day 3 of the festivities was in full swing when Mary noticed that the wine was running low. For a groom to run out of wine was a disgrace. Mary tugged on Jesus' sleeve, and with a mischievous twinkle in her eye she whispered, "They have no more wine."

Jesus replied, "Dear woman, why do you tell me? My time has not come."

As soon as the words escaped Jesus' lips, he felt the nudge from His heavenly Father; the prompting that He had been waiting for His entire life. In a split second, God allowed Mary to flip the switch, to topple the first domino, to ignite the fuse. *It was time.*

Mary turned to the attendants standing nervously by the stone water jars used for ceremonial cleansing. With quiet authority, she nodded toward her Son. "Do whatever He says."

Jesus pointed to six water jars, each with the capacity to hold 20 to 30 gallons of water. "Fill the jars up with water," He instructed.

Quickly, the servants dragged the heavy stone cisterns to the well behind the house and filled them to the brim.

Once they had brought them back to Jesus, He continued. "Now draw some out and take it to the master of the banquet."

Continuing to follow Jesus' instructions, one of the servants dipped his ladle into the jar and poured rich, aromatic red wine into a silver goblet. He couldn't keep his eyes off the miracle he held in his hands. Reverently the servant passed the cup to the master of ceremonies.

"Samuel," the master called out across the court, "you sly dog. Everyone brings out the choice wine first and then the cheaper wine after the guests have had too much to drink; but you have saved the best till now."

The servants were dumbstruck.

Jesus' friends were confused.

Jesus was readied.

Mary was numbed with the reality of what had just taken place. Her time of quiet normalcy was over. She knew that now. What would come next, only God knew.

A Closer Look

And that was the beginning of Jesus' ministry of the miraculous. After 30 years of waiting, God gave Jesus the signal that the time for miracles had begun. Right in the middle of a pack of men— Jesus, Peter, Andrew, James, John, Philip, Nathanael, and the wine stewards—God tapped Mary on the shoulder and chose her to ignite the fuse. Let's take a closer look.

> *On the third day a wedding took place at Cana in Galilee.*
> *Jesus' mother was there, and Jesus and his disciples had*
> *also been invited to the wedding. When the wine was gone,*
> *Jesus' mother said to him, "They have no more wine" (John*
> *2:1-3).*

In first-century Palestine, a wedding celebration lasted for about seven days. The hosts were expected to offer proper hospitality to their guests, and that included a free-flowing supply of wine. To run out of wine was a serious offense and major social embarrassment. And here it was only three days into the festivities when Mary noticed the wine running low.

Mary saw the problem and knew just where to go to remedy the situation.

> *"Dear woman, why do you involve me?" Jesus replied. "My*
> *time has not yet come" (John 2:4).*

If my son called me "woman," I would definitely take offense, but not so in Jesus' day. "Woman" was a polite form of address, and Jesus used it as a term of endearment.

Jesus replied that His "time had not yet come." However, He followed through with Mary's request. Could it be that God tapped Him on the shoulder and assured Him that the time *had* indeed arrived? It appears so.

> *His mother said to the servants, "Do whatever he tells you"*
> *(John 2:5).*

These words have become my life verse. I hope they can be woven into the fabric of your own life as well. They were Mary's mantra. "May it be to me as you have said" became "Do whatever he tells you." Mary isn't just speaking to the servants here. She is speaking to us as well. Do you want to be a woman freed *from an ordinary life* and freed *to an extraordinary purpose*? Then the path is clear. "Do whatever he tells you."

Obedience to God is the key to unlocking the doors to the most exciting life imaginable, but that is no guarantee that our lives will be without pain and struggle.

Let's fast-forward three years and join Mary in one last scene.

Standing at the Foot of the Cross

Mary, probably now in her late forties, was startled from her mending by a pounding on the door. *Who would come here at this time of night?*

"John!" she cried as she peered through the slightly opened door. "What are you doing here? Is it Jesus?"

"Oh, Mary, I don't even know where to begin," he whispered as tears streamed down his agonized face.

"Come in, come in," Mary said as she wrapped her arm around Jesus' closest friend. "Start at the beginning."

"Well, we had a nice Passover dinner on Thursday, but I could tell that Jesus was deeply troubled. There was just a different air about Him. He washed our feet and spoke about leaving us. Something about going to a place we didn't know. Of course, Peter said he would follow Him to the death. You know how Peter boasts."

"Yes, go on."

"After dinner we went to the Garden of Gethsemane. Jesus talked to us as we walked along the road, as if He were a father telling his sons the family secret to success before leaving to go off to war. He was so unsettled and bothered about something. When we arrived at the garden, He told us to pray for Him while He went off to be by Himself. I'm sorry to say that we fell asleep—more than once. At one point I overhead Jesus asking God to *let this cup pass from Him*. When I looked, Jesus had blood dripping from His brow where sweat should have been.

"I was going to ask Him about it, but before I could an angry mob of Romans came and arrested Him!"

"Arrested Him! For what?"

"I don't know. Something about blaspheming. And guess who was at the head of the pack. Judas. I never did trust that man."

John went on to tell Mary of the trial, the flogging, and the ultimate sentencing of execution by crucifixion.

With great resolve, she looked John in the eye and said, "Take me to Him."

It seems that all her life Mary had been trying to save Jesus. She remembered when she and Joseph fled to Egypt to escape Herod's decree to kill all the boy babies under two years old in Bethlehem. She recalled the day she and her sons tried to convince Jesus to come home when she heard rumors that the Pharisees were plotting to kill Him. And now this.

Mary recalled the words of Simeon, the prophet at the temple when she and Joseph took their baby to be consecrated to the Lord: "This child is destined to cause the falling and rising of many in Israel, and to be a sign that will be spoken against, so that the thoughts of many hearts will be revealed. And a sword will pierce your own soul too" (Luke 2:34-35). This was the sword Simeon had spoken of, piercing her heart with a pain only a mother could understand.

Arriving on the Via de la Rosa, Mary watched with horror as her firstborn Son trudged through the jeering crowd. His flesh hung in shreds, torn by floggings of the Roman metal-tipped whip; His body was crusted with dried blood and mud from collapsing under the weight of the cross tied to His back; and streaks of crimson cut furrows down His face from the crown of thorns pressed into His forehead.

When Jesus reached the place where His mother stood among the crowd, He raised His head to meet her gaze. A thousand thoughts passed between them without a single spoken word. She was there, just as she had been all along.

Later, as He hung on the cross, Jesus breathed His final parting words.

"Dear woman, here is your son," Jesus moaned as He nodded toward John.

And then to John He said, "Here is your mother."

Even in His last breaths, Jesus' concern was for this chosen girl from Nazareth—His mother—Mary.

A Closer Look

Mary had been there all along. She was there to hear the babe's first cry in Bethlehem and there to hear the Savior's final breath at Calvary. If we dare, let's join her at the foot of the cross and take a closer took.

> *Near the cross of Jesus stood his mother, his mother's sister,*
> *Mary the wife of Clopas, and Mary Magdalene (John 19:25).*

We don't have a lot of information about Mary at the foot of the cross, except that she was there—standing below her flesh-torn, blood-drenched, physically battered, precious Son. She heard the hammer hit the nails, saw the Roman spear pierce His side, felt the labor of His breathing. As His heart burst, her chest ached. For six hours she watched Him die. Pierced. How perfectly that word described her at this moment. The sword that had hung over her head for 33 years now pierced her heart.

It must have seemed like an eternity since a symphony of angels announced His birth. Now a cacophony of accusers hurled insults and accusations. "Crucify Him!" the savage rabble demanded. "He saved others, but He can't save Himself," the chief priests and elders taunted.

Where are those angels now, she must have thought. If she could have peered into the spiritual realm, she would have found them hovering low, silent in full armor array.

It is sometimes difficult to envision God's presence surrounding the tragedies in our lives. Somehow the two don't seem to be able to co-exist in our minds. It is almost incomprehensible to picture the angles standing by while mere humans taunted and tortured the Son of God. What do we do when life doesn't make sense? We remember.

Mary remembered Gabriel's announcement.

Mary remembered Elizabeth's welcome.

Mary remembered Joseph's dreams.

Mary remembered the shepherds' arrival.

Mary remembered the magis' gifts.

Mary remembered Simeon's prophecy.

Mary remembered Anna's words.

Mary remembered the 12-year-old boy in His Father's house.

Mary remembered the water transformed to wine.

Mary remembered the miracles.

Mary remembered the teaching.

Mary remembered the healings.

Mary remembered.

After the shepherds' visit in the stables that first Christmas evening, Luke tells us, "Mary treasured up all these things and pondered them in her heart" (Luke 2:19). No doubt her thoughts returned to that treasure chest of memories for the reassurance she so needed. The events of Jesus' life slipped through her mind like beads on a string with the knot of faith tied securely at the end.

And, friend, that is what we must do. The Bible tells us that in Christ "are hidden all the treasures of wisdom and knowledge" (Colossians 2:3). When we treasure God's Word in our hearts, just as Mary did in hers, it calms the waves of doubt during the storms of life. The storm may not be removed, but God's Word will help us to hold steady as the difficulties of life toss us to and fro.

> *When Jesus saw his mother there, and the disciple whom he loved standing nearby, he said to his mother, "Dear woman, here is your son," and to the disciple, "Here is your mother." From that time on, this disciple took her into his home (John 19:26-27).*

Jesus thought of Mary till the very end. Some of His last words on the cross were to her. Once again Jesus pulls Mary from the crowd and places her center stage. God's spotlight shone on this ordinary girl from Nazareth, and we savor her faithfulness, her resolve to obedience one last time.

Mary was not spared the pain and shame of having a son executed as a common criminal, but her identity did not rest on her role as a mother of a tortured son. Jesus, her Savior, set her free from insignificance and placed her firmly among the disciples who were chosen to change the world.

Freed from an Ordinary Life

Mary. Who was she? A seemingly insignificant teenage girl from Nazareth who opened the door for all women to obey God with total surrender—no matter what the cost. "May it be to me as you have said" becomes our battle cry.

We tend to look at the Mary of Christmas and Easter, but there was a whole lot of living in between. From the cradle to the cross, God used this woman to nurture His Son, to encourage His Son, and shore up His Son in the face of death. She began by leading her young Son by the hand, and she ended her journey with Him leading her by the heart.

Author Carolyn Custis James described Mary so well:

> She was Jesus' first disciple. She had been one from the beginning—as a teenager. She was a hearer and doer of God's Word. Faced with a hard and costly choice, she blazed a path of faith and courage for all women—young and old—and demonstrated the power of a woman who will risk everything to advance God's cause...She offers teenage girls today a stronger role model than some of the alternatives that beckon them. She sets an example for those of us who are adults too. Mary was the first to believe and lay down her life for the gospel. She was the first to leave all to follow Jesus, first to love him and minister to his body, first to hear and treasure his words, the first to share in his sufferings. Incredible as it sounds, for a brief time Mary had Jesus all to herself. She was his first disciple.[2]

God didn't *need* Mary in order for Jesus to appear on this earth. He created Adam from a little dust and spit. God *chose* for His Son to enter this world through the womb of a woman. But she was more than an incubator for the Son of God. Giving birth was not her only role. She was the first believer. The first follower. The first disciple. The first to hold Him. The first to mourn Him. She was God's chosen instrument to inaugurate Jesus' ministry as she spoke, "Do whatever he tells you."

Mary was the mother of a murdered son and the widow of a deceased husband. It would have been easy for her to fall back into insignificance at such a fate filled with broken dreams. But that is not where we see her last. In her parting scene in the grand drama of her life, we see Mary with the disciples waiting for the promised Holy Spirit and her next assignment in life. She knew who she was. She was a chosen child of God set free to serve in a mighty army of believers and impact the world with the gospel.

Free to Fulfill an Extraordinary Purpose

In the book of Acts, we meet Mary one last time. After Jesus' resurrection, He addressed the disciples before His ascent to take His seat at the right hand of the Father. He instructed them to wait for the promised Holy Spirit, reassured them that He would return again, and commissioned them to share the gospel to the ends of the earth. Then Jesus was taken up before their very eyes, and the group headed to Jerusalem to wait (Acts 1:1-14).

So who was among this commissioned group of disciples who gathered in the upper room to wait for the promised Holy Spirit? Peter, John, James, Andrew, Philip, Thomas, Bartholomew, Matthew, James, Simon, Judas son of James, the women, Mary the mother of Jesus, and His brothers. Hold everything! The women? Yes, the women. We'll find out more about those gals a bit later. Mary? Yes, Mary. For centuries the religious leaders had been an all-boys club. But now a fresh wind blew in to change the scenery of the new order called "the church." Jesus' parting words commissioned both men and women to spread the gospel to the ends of the earth.

Mary, the mother of Jesus, was among the disciples. She was a disciple, a learner, a follower. She was commissioned with the rest to spread the gospel "in Jerusalem, and in all Judea and Samaria, and to the ends of the earth" (Acts 1:8). And while we don't meet up with this incredible woman again, we can be sure she did just that.

Mary was among the collective prophecies of Joel: "In the last days, God says, I will pour out my Spirit on all people. Your sons and daughters will prophesy, your young men will see visions, your old men will dream dreams. Even on my servants, *both men and women,* I will pour out my Spirit in those days, and they will prophesy'" (Acts 2:17-18; see also Joel 2:28-29).

We have to be careful not to worship Mary. Jesus didn't. When someone from a crowd yelled, "Blessed is the mother who gave you birth and nursed you," Jesus answered, "Blessed rather are those who hear the word of God and obey it" (Luke 11:27-28).

Perhaps the most remarkable character trait of Mary, the one we can grasp with both hands and soar with her to great heights, is her radical obedience. From the very beginning, Mary's response to God's call on her life rings through the ages: "I am the Lord's servant…May it be to me as you have said" (Luke 1:38). When that is our response to God's call, we will indeed lead extraordinary lives filled with great exploits for the kingdom.

Yes, God chose Mary. Yes, God chose you. He has freed us from insignificance, and the key to access that freedom lies in Jesus' words: "Blessed rather are those who hear the word of God and obey it." That is where our significance lies.

That type of obedience flows from a relationship of trust. It is not a burden or a "have to," but a joy and a "want to." It is not obedience simply because the Bible says so, but an adventure because we link arms with Jesus and follow Him into great purpose. This is a place where our simple water is transformed into the robust wine of life.

God has great plans for all of us. "Things which eye has not seen and ear has not heard, and which have not entered the heart of man, all that God has prepared for those who love Him" (1 Corinthians 2:9 NASB). As Mary has shown us, God sets the offer before us, but

He will not force His plan on anyone. We have to choose and say yes to Him. That, my friend, is the key to abundant life.

God freed Mary from an ordinary life and freed her to fulfill an extraordinary purpose. He called an ordinary girl center stage, and she willingly walked forward to take her place. I'm so glad she did.

Blessed is she who has believed that what the
Lord has said to her will be accomplished!

LUKE 1:45

3

The Fearless Follower (Mary Magdalene)

Freed from Spiritual Darkness
Freed to Share God's Light to the World

She was just a normal little girl frolicking about the house, toying with the goats, and sticking her fingers in her mother's rising dough. After her father died, Mary's mother tried her best to raise the child on what little her husband had left behind. But when puberty began to bloom, a poisonous weed began to take root in Mary's mind. With each passing year, her behavior grew more and more erratic.

Often she was seen banging her head against the wall of their modest home, screaming curses to unseen shadows, crawling like an animal through the yard, and cutting her arms with sharp-edged stones. Mary's mother was almost relieved when the deranged young woman ran away to live among the tombs. "Now I won't have to deal with her craziness," her mother breathed.

Mary Magdalene was a demon-possessed lunatic—unwanted, unclean, untouchable, and unapproachable. But all that was about to change.

"Peter," Jesus said as He led the group of men toward the cemetery on the fringes of Magdala, "I need to stop by here for a moment."

"But why?" John questioned. "Do you have a relative's grave you wish to visit?"

"Not a physically dead relative, but a spiritually dead sister who needs Me."

With confused looks on their faces, Jesus' followers knew not to argue with His travel plans. It seemed He always had an agenda that they knew not of.

As soon as the band of disciples neared the tombs, a half-dressed woman in tattered rags bolted from the brush.

"We know who You are," the woman hissed. "You are the Son of God. What do You want with us?"

The disciples recoiled at the sight and stench of this mad woman, but Jesus drew near. Certainly this was not the sister He mentioned. With a shout Jesus directed His words toward the woman but rebuked the demons within. "Come out of her!"

The woman fell to the ground in a violent seizure. After a few moments of bloodcurdling screams and obscene curses, she lay perfectly still.

"Is she dead?" James asked.

"No, My friend," Jesus replied. "She is actually more alive than she has ever been."

Jesus knelt down beside her, brushed the hair from her eyes, and extended His hand. "Mary, daughter of Abraham, rise to newness of life."

The disciples stared wide eyed as Mary stood to her feet and in her right mind. Her crazy countenance was replaced by perfect peace.

"Thank You, thank You," she cried as tears of freedom and joy coursed down her weathered cheeks.

Jesus turned to walk away to His next assignment, but rather than stand and stare in awe, Mary ran to follow. The disciples waited for Jesus to send her away. They were quite surprised when He did just the opposite and motioned for her to come along. From that day on, she would remain among the disciples to do whatever she could to further the ministry of Jesus.

A Closer Look

We don't know much about Mary Magdalene's encounter with Jesus and her deliverance from demons. A closer look at her emancipation only allows us to examine one solitary sentence. "The Twelve were with him, and also some women who had been cured of evil spirits and diseases: Mary (called Magdalene) from whom seven demons had come out" (Luke 8:1-2).

The Bible gives us many snapshots of men and women posessed by demons. They threw themselves into fire (Matthew 17:15), thrashed on the ground (Luke 4:35), violently convulsed (Matthew 17:15), cried out (Mark 5:5; Luke 4:33-34; 8:28), exhibited unrestrainable superhuman strength (Luke 8:29; Mark 5:4), and foamed at the mouth (Luke 9:39). Some cut themselves with sharp objects (Mark 5:5), ran about naked (Luke 8:27), and lived among the tombs (Luke 8:27). Some were blind (Matthew 12:22) and others mute (Matthew 12:22; Luke 11:14). While we don't know the exact manifestations Mary Magdalene exhibited, we can assume she lived a dark and deranged existence controlled by demons that haunted her day and night. Let's take a closer look at Mary to glean from the few verses we do have.

> *After this, Jesus traveled about from one town and village to another, proclaiming the good news of the kingdom of God (Luke 8:1).*

After what? That's a good question. Since Jesus' time of ministry had begun, Jesus had been baptized by His cousin John in the Jordan River, tempted by His enemy Satan in the wilderness, and empowered by the Holy Spirit to perform miracles in urban centers and small villages alike. Jesus had chosen His 12 key disciples, raised a widow's son from the dead, and taught the multitudes.

Jesus continued His travels proclaiming the gospel, which actually means "good news." Jesus taught the masses the good news of grace, repentance, forgiveness of sins, and the promise of eternal life. He explained new spiritual truths with everyday stories people could understand.

> *The Twelve were with him, and also some women who*
> *had been cured of evil spirits and diseases: Mary (called*
> *Magdalene) from whom seven demons had come out;*
> *Joanna the wife of Cuza, the manager of Herod's household;*
> *Susanna; and many others (Luke 8:1-2).*

For most of my life I pictured Jesus traveling about with His 12 disciples. After all, isn't that the picture in the Sunday school books? It was only recently that the landscape in my mind changed dramatically. I had to walk over to the easel in my mind and paint a new picture on a fresh canvas. Jesus didn't travel about with only the 12 men. Luke lets us know that there were women who traveled with them as well: Mary Magdalene, Joanna, Susanna, and many others.

"...and many others." I just love that. These were women who had been healed, delivered, saved, and empowered by Jesus. Where have they been all my life? They have been there all along, but somehow I missed their influence and impact on Jesus' earthly ministry. I allowed ancient artists to paint the pictures of Jesus and His entourage in my mind rather than Scripture. But no more.

So who was Mary Magdalene? Of all the women in the Bible, perhaps she is surrounded with the most mystery, presumption, and speculation. We're not given a lot of information except where she was from and what she had been like before she met Jesus.

Eight out of nine times in the Bible when Mary Magdalene is mentioned with a grouping of other women, her name appears first. In that culture, "the order of naming indicated the order of importance."[1] More than 50 percent of the women in Palestine in Jesus' day were named either Mary or Salome.[2] That's a lot of Marys, and it is understandable that they have been confused. But Mary Magdalene "was clearly a woman of prominence, not to be confused with any other Mary in the New Testament. Everybody knew which woman you were talking about when you said, 'Mary Magdalene.'"[3]

We also know that Mary was from Magdala, one of nine cities on the western shore of the Sea of Galilee.[4] It stood along the ancient road from Nazareth to Damascus, not far south of Capernaum.[5] Though its name does not appear on modern day maps, Magdala was in the heartland of Jesus' ministry.

Throughout history, Mary Magdalene's identity has been confused with other women in the New Testament. Some have suggested that she was the sinful woman who anointed Jesus' feet at the Pharisee's dinner party (Luke 7:37). But Luke tells the story of the woman anointing Jesus' feet in chapter 7 and then introduces Mary Magdalene for the first time in chapter 8. Nowhere is Mary Magdalene ever mentioned as a "sinful woman." She was simply a woman from whom Jesus cast seven demons. These are two entirely different women, regardless of what the Renaissance painters have portrayed.

Some have even suggested that Mary Magdalene was the woman caught in adultery. But I don't know of many men who would be drawn to a woman possessed by seven demons, especially from what we've learned about the typical manifestations of other demoniacs. Not once in the New Testament do we read of Jesus delivering someone from demons and then saying, "Your sins are forgiven." Nowhere does Jesus use the word "sinful" to describe someone possessed by demons. Another clue that these two women are not one and the same is found in Jesus' final words to the woman caught in adultery. His final charge was "go in peace" (Luke 7:50), not "come follow Me."

In *The Da Vinci Code*, novelist Dan Brown suggested that Mary Magdalene was married to Jesus and they had a child together. Brown's story line alleges that the "beloved apostle" in Leonardo Da Vinci's masterpiece *The Last Supper* was none other than Mary Magdalene and not the apostle John. Friend, Jesus was not married and He did not have a child. Important information such as that would not have been omitted from the Scriptures.

Unfortunately, for many years art was "the Bible for the illiterate"[6] and the cause of many myths of Mary Magdalene being passed down through the centuries. Aren't you glad we live in a day where we can hold a Bible in our hands and learn God's truth directly from Him?

Here's what we know: Mary Magdalene was a woman possessed and controlled by seven demons, but at some point she had an encounter with Jesus, who delivered her from the clutches of Satan and into the hands of God. From that point on, I believe Mary's mission in life was to do what she could to serve her Savior, Lord, Healer, Redeemer, and Teacher. And how did she do that?

> *These women were helping to support them out of their own means (Luke 8:3).*

Like most women, I sense that Mary and the other women did what needed doing. They saw a need and met it. They supported Jesus and His ministry financially, personally, and spiritually. The word "helping" is from the Greek word *diaokinos,* which is sometimes translated "minister." It is where we get the word "deacon" or "deaconess."

"Out of their own means" has also been translated "considerable means" (MSG), "private means" (NASB), and "their own resources" (NEB). We aren't told where these women obtained their sizable nest eggs, but simply that they were generous women of means.

These women also sat at Jesus' feet as He taught, ignoring cultural and religious man-made boundaries that prohibited women from sitting under the teaching of a rabbi. When Mary Magdalene met the resurrected Jesus at the empty garden tomb, she addressed Him as "Teacher." She didn't call Him "Healer," "Provider," or "Ruler." Jesus is indeed all that and more, but her first instinct was to address Him in a way she knew best—He was her teacher.

It seems these women were just as willing to go against the social norms to serve Jesus as Jesus was willing to cross gender boundaries to invite them. I'm so glad they said yes. And as for Mary Magdalene, her most important assignment was yet to come.

On the Third Day

In a matter of three years, Jesus had turned the world upside down. His followers had great expectations for how His earthly reign would play out. And even though Jesus had tried to prepare them, they were taken completely off guard by His arrest and crucifixion. When His body was sealed away in that darkened tomb, their hopes and dreams were sealed away as well. Mary was among those whose shattered dreams lay scattered under the cross. Little did she know that the best was yet to come. Let's join her in the wee hours on that Sunday morning so many years ago.

It was still dark as Mary arose from yet another sleepless night of tossing and turning. The horrific events of Friday's crucifixion played over and over in her mind. In just a few short hours, her life had been turned upside down. Her hopes and dreams drained out with every drop of Jesus' precious blood. When He uttered the words, "It is finished," she felt that her life was over as well.

Mary had pinned all her hopes and dreams on Jesus. He had given her a new mind, a new purpose, and a new life. But now that He was gone, the chains of the past rattled in the background. Fear was knocking at the door. Would she get sick again? Would the demons return? What would she do?

"I can't believe this happened," she cried to herself as she paced the cold hard floor. "What am I going to do without Him?" Then, like the rising sun, a thought rose in the sadness of her mind. Suddenly, Mary knew what she had to do. An unexplainable urge led her to the box of spices on the kitchen shelf and out the door. "I must go to Him," she whispered. Mary gathered Mary the mother of James, Joanna, and Salome, and the foursome made their way to the tomb before the first stream of sunlight streaked the sky.

A predawn mist hovered over the garden surrounding the tomb where Jesus' body had been laid days earlier. "Mary," Salome asked, "who will roll the stone away from the entrance so we can attend to Jesus' body?"

"I don't know, Salome. We'll worry about that when we get there."

Broken and shattered, the women moved in deep sorrow and mourning over the death of their beloved Savior and Lord. *Why?* Mary silently cried. *Why did God allow this to happen?*

As the women approached the tomb, something was amiss. No guards and, more important, no stone. Mary ran to the entrance of the open tomb and peered inside to find it empty. She crumpled to the ground in a heap. "Who would have done such a thing? Isn't it enough that they tortured, beat, and crucified this innocent man? Why would they have stolen His body?" The other women stood together in a huddle of tears, clinging to one another in despair.

"I must go and tell the others," Mary said as she dried her tears and dashed from the empty tomb. Off she ran to tell the disciples.

"They took Him!" Mary cried breathlessly as she burst through the door of the room where some of the disciples were hiding. "His body is gone!"

Without asking any questions, Peter jumped up and bolted from the room. A much younger and more agile John followed close behind and eventually passed his older friend.

"He's not here," John whispered as he peered inside the opening of the cave. "His body is gone."

A moment later, a breathless Peter arrived. He didn't stop at the mouth of the cave but rushed in.

"Look," John said to his winded friend. "Over there in the corner."

A ray of sunlight pierced the darkness and pointed their attention to Jesus' empty burial cloths. Strips of linen that had once covered Jesus' head now lay neatly folded in a corner.

"What happened here? What does this mean?" they asked one another.

Peter and John went back to report their findings to the other disciples, while Mary Magdalene stayed behind. Deep guttural cries of mourning pierced the quiet as she knelt by the empty tomb. Suddenly, a beam of light caught her attention. There, at the spot where Jesus' body had been laid, sat two glistening angels clothed in white.

"Woman, why are you crying?" one of the angels asked.

"They have taken my Master," Mary replied through her tears. "I don't know where they have taken Him."

Hearing a rustling in the myrtle bushes behind her, Mary turned her head. She felt a presence and discerned she was not alone. Someone was in the garden with her.

"Woman, why are you weeping?" the man asked.

Thinking the man was the gardener she continued. "Sir," she cried, "if you know where they have taken Jesus, would you please tell me so that I can take care of Him?"

Then Jesus said one simple word: "Mary."

At the sound of her name, Mary recognized the risen Lord. She jumped with a start.

"Rabboni!" she cried. The one who had taught her, who had instructed her, who had loved her was alive!

Mary fell on her knees and clung to Jesus' feet with a blending of tears and laughter. There was so much she wanted to say, to ask. But her words were lost in emotion.

"You have to let me go," Jesus said softly, "for I haven't yet returned to My Father. Please go to My brothers and tell them, 'I will soon be returning to our Father and God.'"

With a smile that put the rising sun to shame, Mary turned and ran to tell the others the good news. Jesus had risen, just like He said.

"I have seen Him! I have seen the Lord!"

A Closer Look

Jesus knew it was coming. He tried to warn the disciples. Death loomed in the air with swirls of bloodthirsty hatred circling the Son of God. But somehow the disciples didn't understand the imminence of Jesus' crucifixion, and they certainly didn't comprehend the promise of His resurrection. Mary Magdalene didn't understand it either. However, she was there until the end...and at the new beginning for us all.

After Jesus' arrest, His 11 surprised disciples scattered like church mice when the lights come on. But not Mary Magdalene. She watched in horror as His beaten body was stripped naked, nailed to the cruel Roman cross, and displayed before the gawking crowd. She stood close by as His precious blood dripped from His thorn-pierced brow and on to the cursed ground. Mary watched closely when His lifeless body was lowered from the cross and followed quietly when they laid Him in the borrowed tomb. We get no stories of Mary Magdalene running away from the authorities, hiding behind locked doors, or denying her association with Jesus from curious bystanders. Is it any wonder that Jesus chose this loyal disciple to be the first one to see His resurrected form?

Jesus' resurrection was the most pivotal point in all of history, and yet He waited until Peter and John had left the empty tomb before He made His presence known to one lone woman. Jesus was standing center stage, and He extended His hand for Mary Magdalene to join Him front and center. Let's go back to the Scriptures and take a closer look at the most important event in history.

> *Near the cross of Jesus stood his mother, his mother's sister,*
> *Mary the wife of Clopas, and Mary Magdalene (John 19:25).*

While most of the disciples scattered in fear at the arrest and crucifixion of Jesus, Mary Magdalene, along with some of the other leading women, stood at the cross until the end. They heard the low moans of His suffering, watched the streams of blood splatter the ground, and saw the last beat of his broken heart.

> *Joseph brought some linen cloth, took down the body,*
> *wrapped it in the linen, and placed it in a tomb cut out of*
> *rock. Then he rolled a stone against the entrance of the tomb.*
> *Mary Magdalene and Mary the mother of Joses saw where he*
> *was laid (Mark 15:46-47).*

As the crowd of observers and mourners parted the scene, two remained: Mary, the mother of James and Joses, and Mary Magdalene.

They were there when two men, Joseph of Arimathea and Nicodemus, took Jesus' body down from the cross, prepared Him for burial, and placed Him in the garden tomb.

> *When the Sabbath was over, Mary Magdalene, Mary the*
> *mother of James, and Salome brought spices so that they*
> *might go to anoint Jesus' body. Very early on the first day of*
> *the week, just after sunrise, they were on their way to the*
> *tomb and they asked each other, "Who will roll the stone*
> *away from the entrance of the tomb?" (Mark 16:1-3).*

The women "worried out loud to each other" (MSG) about how they were going to move the stone away from the opening of the cave. This was no small task. The burial chamber was "sealed with a cut, disk-shaped stone that rolled in a slot cut into the rock. The slot was on an incline, making the grave easy to seal but difficult to open: several men might be needed to roll the stone back."[7]

> *But when they looked up, they saw that the stone, which was*
> *very large, had been rolled away. As they entered the tomb,*
> *they saw a young man dressed in a white robe sitting on*
> *the right side, and they were alarmed. "Don't be alarmed,"*
> *he said. "You are looking for Jesus the Nazarene, who was*
> *crucified. He has risen! He is not here. See the place where*
> *they laid him. But go, tell his disciples and Peter, 'He is going*
> *ahead of you into Galilee. There you will see him, just as he*
> *told you'" (Mark 16:4-7).*

John tells us more about what happened next. The women did indeed tell the disciples what they saw. Matthew tells us that they "hurried away from the tomb, afraid yet filled with joy" (Matthew 28:8). Another translation says, "with fear and great joy" (AMP). I can see our sisters now—laughing and crying, relieved and apprehensive, running and skipping. Finally, they reached the boys and shouted the news!

Peter and John rushed back to the tomb and found it just as the women had testified—empty. John tells us he "saw and believed"

(John 20:8). However, the sentence lacks a direct object, which means it doesn't tell us *what* he believed. The next sentence gives us a clue. "They still did not understand from Scripture that Jesus had to rise from the dead" (John 20:9). So what did John believe? He believed that the tomb was empty. Theologian Matthew Henry wrote: "One cannot but be amazed at the stupidity of these disciples."[8] I didn't say it. Mr. Henry did.

Well, Peter and John "went back to their homes" (verse 10). This is further proof the disciples didn't believe Mary's report that Jesus had risen from the dead. If they had believed her, they would have been celebrating and looking for Him rather than slinking back home in defeat.

Mary stood outside the tomb crying (John 20:11).

While the men returned to their homes, Mary Magdalene stayed behind at the empty tomb weeping. Author Liz Higgs describes Mary's anguish:

> Every widow among us understands that sense of utter loss. The endless empty hours, the feeling of purposelessness, the unanswered questions, the unfinished business, the longings that threaten to crush us to dust. Mary Magdalene's heart surely felt as vacant and gaping as the empty tomb before her. Her tear-filled grief was like the faint fragrance of myrrh, scenting the air with sorrow.[9]

> *As she wept, she bent over to look into the tomb and saw two angels in white, seated where Jesus' body had been, one at the head and the other at the foot (John 20:11-12).*

Mary saw the two angels in the very same position as the angels on the Ark of the Covenant—one at the head and one at the foot. I wonder if she drew the parallel between the Ark of the Covenant, which was a shadow of the reality she was seeing this very day. And while the angels before her did speak, it was another voice behind her that stirs our hearts.

> *"Woman," he said, "why are you crying? Who it is you are looking for?" Thinking he was the gardener, she said, "Sir, if you have carried him away, tell me where you have put him, and I will get him." Jesus said to her, "Mary" (John 20:15-16).*

My heart just skips a beat every time I read these words. I see myself weeping with Mary as she is down on her knees with gut-wrenching sorrow pouring from her soul. All her dreams—shattered. They died with Jesus on the cross and were sealed away in the cold, dark tomb. Like a sweeping tidal wave, the empty tomb erased the most important three years of her life...and then all that changed with one word. "Mary."

As soon as He said her name, Mary knew it was Jesus.

Earlier Jesus had taught, "I am the good shepherd; I know my sheep and my sheep know me...My sheep listen to my voice; I know them, and they follow me" (John 10:14,27). When the Shepherd spoke her name, this precious lamb recognized Him right away.

And what was the first word the risen Savior spoke? "Woman." Don't you love it! Jesus came to set women free from societal and religious oppression of His day. He honored women. He respected women. He appointed women. His first spoken words after His resurrection were directed to one of us—and in a sense it was meant for *all* of us.

> *She turned toward him and cried out in Aramaic, "Rabboni!" (which means Teacher). Jesus said, "Do not hold on to me, for I have not yet returned to the Father. Go instead to my brothers and tell them, 'I am returning to my Father and your Father, to my God and your God'" (John 20:16-17).*

What did Mary do when she realized that Jesus was alive? The same thing I would do if I realized that someone I loved who was presumed dead suddenly appeared. I'd grab him or her and hang on for dear life! The Greek word for "hold on to me" actually me~

"to clutch or grip."[10] One translation states "stop clinging to Me" (NASB). "Not only did she need to release her grip on his clothing, she also needed to let go of her old definition of who Jesus was. Her friend and teacher had suddenly become a great deal more than a righteous man rooted to her time and place. He was now a risen Savior for all mankind, for all time."[11]

Mary needed to let go of Jesus because He was sending her on a special assignment. She had places to go and people to see! "Just as God chose Mary of Bethlehem to bring the baby Jesus into the world, so God chose Mary of Magdala to bring news of the risen Christ to the world."[12]

> Mary Magdalene went to the disciples with the news: "I have seen the Lord!" And she told them that he had said these things to her (John 20:18).

All four Gospels agree that Mary was the first to witness the resurrection and the first to tell the news. Peter and John were two of Jesus' closest friends. In John's Gospel, John refers to himself as "the one Jesus loved" (John 20:2). And yet, when Peter and John arrived at the empty tomb, Jesus kept quiet. He waited until they had gone and Mary Magdalene was alone.

Why? I don't know all the reasons why He did it. I just know that He did. During a time in history when women were not allowed to testify in court, when they were considered unreliable witnesses, God appointed Mary Magdalene the primary eyewitness of the most significant event in all of history. A woman!

Mary is often referred to as the "disciple to the disciples" or, as Augustine described her, the "apostle of the apostles." Not only was she the first to witness Jesus' resurrection, but she was also the first to proclaim it. This fact in itself is proof of the authenticity of Jesus' resurrection. No man or religious leader of Jesus' day would dare come up with a story that Jesus appeared first to a woman. If it were fabricated, writers would have certainly chosen a man.

Freed from Spiritual Darkness

While most of us have probably not experienced spiritual darkness to the extent of our sister Mary Magdalene, we have all lived it to some degree. The Bible tells us that before we come to Christ, we live in darkness (1 Peter 2:9). Not only were we *in* darkness, we *were* darkness. Paul wrote, "For you were once darkness, but now you are light in the Lord" (Ephesians 5:8).

Like Mary Magdalene, we have been set free from spiritual darkness. "He [the Father] has rescued us from the dominion of darkness and brought us into the kingdom of the Son he loves" (Colossians 1:13). We have more in common with our sister Mary Magdalene than we might have originally thought.

In most cases, men and women with physical illnesses came to Jesus. They traveled miles, bore holes through rooftops, grabbed at His clothes, and fell pleading at His feet. But when it came to those possessed by demons, Jesus went to them or a relative came begging for help. We can safely assume that Jesus went to Mary Magdalene. One day, she was Jesus' assignment. God had her name written on Jesus' celestial Day-Timer. "Long before we first heard of Christ… he had his eye on us, had designs on us for glorious living, part of the overall purpose he is working out in everything and everyone" (Ephesians 1:11-12 MSG).

God had a plan for Mary Magdalene, and the enemy couldn't stop it no matter how hard he tried. She wasn't seeking Him, but "Jesus' strong arm reached into the black darkness that engulfed her and pulled her out to safety anyway."[13] He set her free from spiritual darkness, restored her dignity, and gave her a place in His personal ministry team.

Freed to Share God's Light to the World

Regardless of all the supposition surrounding the name of Mary Magdalene, the facts show that she was one of the most significant women in the New Testament. She enjoyed a personal, ongoing relationship with Jesus. While most women had an encounter with

Jesus that changed their lives, Mary had an encounter plus a face-to-face relationship that continued beyond His death and resurrection to the Father. She played a significant role in Jesus' life and ministry, and yet we only catch glimpses of her ministry and leadership among the disciples. This woman, once possessed by demons, becomes a disciple of Jesus who traveled about with the chosen 12.

Why? I'm not sure. If I were to make a list of possibilities, then I would be doing what writers have been doing for centuries and muddying the waters even more. What we do know for sure is that Jesus allowed, or rather invited, Mary Magdalene to come along with Him and His disciples. All four of the Gospel accounts include Mary Magdalene with Jesus' most devout followers, and she is present at some of the most pivotal points in history.

In those days, a Jewish rabbi would have never approved of a woman traveling about with a group of men. And yet we see Jesus the Liberator including Mary Magdalene in His ministry team.

When God said in Genesis 2:18 that "it is not good for the man to be alone," He meant, "It is not good for the man to be alone." Could it be that Jesus was teaching the disciples the value of women's input during this time when females had been secluded and excluded from anything of religious merit? The church was not meant to be an all-male institution, but a blending of male and female image bearers working together to spread the gospel and build the body of Christ. Jesus, our example setter, was showing them how.

Jesus ignored cultural norms that treated women as second-class, low-life creatures. Women who had been previously kept sequestered in their homes, now struck out on a radical mission to change the world.

Jesus came to set women free. Free from and free to. He set Mary Magdalene free from seven demons and free to become a vital part of His ministry team. She is a breathtaking example that our pasts do not determine our future.

I hope you are seeing yourself through Jesus' eyes. I hope you are seeing your potential to impact your part of the world with the gospel. I hope you are getting a taste of the incredible significance you have as a child of God and an ambassador for Christ.

Women in the church have been far too timid in their approach to ministry. They have felt unsure where they belong. While most agree that God gives spiritual gifts to every believer, they are often unsure how those gifts are to be used. Does God give women the gift of teaching? Absolutely. And yet some feel that they can only teach a certain demographic, mainly three-and-a-half-feet and under.

I know I may be ruffling some feathers here. Jesus did that too. I am so thankful for the few and the brave who have ventured out of their comfort zones to accept the call of God on their lives.

Amy Carmichael left the safe harbor of Europe and traveled to India to open orphanages for abused girls.[14] By the beginning of the twentieth century, there were 40 evangelical missionary organizations led by women.[15] Hudson Taylor's wife, Maria, led groups of women missionaries deep into China on long preaching journeys where no Westerner had ever gone.[16] Lottie Moon, perhaps one of the most famous Baptist women missionaries, trained indigenous pastors in Northern China in the late 1800s and was extremely successful in evangelism and church planting.[17] And these are just a few. How proud I am of my sisters who have answered the call to join Jesus on His ministry team.

Jesus broke the chains that had women bound. This carpenter from Nazareth demolished culturally built walls and constructed doorways for women to walk through. He gave them expanded roles in ministry and validated them as leaders. He called them out from being mere stagehands and onto center stage to assume leading roles.

Mary Magdalene had been isolated from the healthy, but now she was integrated back into society. She had been an ostracized outcast, but now she was a key witness to the most important event in history. She had been rejected by society, but now she was recognized by God. She had been ignored by the townsfolk, but now she was incorporated into the very fabric of Jesus' earthly ministry.

She had been a spiritual conduit for evil, but now she was a spiritual powerhouse for good. She had been viewed as a loser, but now she was transformed into an amazing leader.

Interestingly, "Magdala" is from the Hebrew word *migdol*, which means "a tower or watchtower."[18] How beautifully those words describe our beloved sister, for she was truly the watchtower who first spotted the resurrected Jesus and shouted the news to anyone who would listen.

On that first Easter morning, when God rolled away the stone, it was not just to let Jesus out, but to let the women in. He still rolls away the stones to allow us to enter places we never dreamed possible, see miracles we never thought feasible, and minister to people we never imagined reachable.

And, friend, that is good news. Jesus comes to each of us in our own particular darkness and delivers us into His light. In the garden, Jesus gave Mary the authority and the mandate to go and tell the good news of His resurrection. He gives us the same authority and mandate today. God still calls women center stage and commissions us to go and tell the most significant event in all of history. "I have seen the LORD!"

> *This is what the LORD says: "In the time of my*
> *favor I will answer you, and in the day of salvation*
> *I will help you…to say to the captive, 'Come*
> *out,' and to those in darkness, 'Be free!'"*
>
> ISAIAH 49:9-10

The Chronically Ill Bold Believer

Freed from Hopelessness
Freed to Share the Hope Within Her

Gone. All gone."

For 12 long years, she had been bleeding. More than 4380 days. Lydia had gone from doctor to doctor to stop the flow, but as the years progressed her condition only worsened. Each day was a reminder of the emptiness she felt as her very life ebbed from her body.

"I've lost my family, my friends, my energy, and now all my money. My womanhood, the ability to conceive and suckle a child at my breast, flows out of my body and leaves me a barren wasteland. And the pain? The constant cramping feels as though my womb is being squeezed by an invisible hand.

"'Unclean.' That's what the priests say I am. No one is supposed to even touch me unless they are willing to go through a cleansing process afterward. The house I live in, the chair I sit in, the utensils I cook with—all ceremonially unclean. Oh, how I long for a human touch. A hug. A kiss. A pat on the back. A baby's cheek against my own.

"Oh, God," Lydia prayed. "There is nothing else for me to do.

I've tried everything. Only a miracle will set me free from this life of isolation."

God smiled down at this daughter of Abraham and noticed her name on Jesus' celestial Day-Timer. Today was the day.

Sitting all alone in a darkened room, she heard a ruckus outside her window.

"It's Jesus!" someone shouted. "Jesus is coming!"

Jesus. Maybe He could heal me. I know I'm not supposed to go out in public. And I certainly cannot speak to this man or any man on the street. What can I do?

Quickly, she devised a plan. She wrapped a veil around her face with only enough of an opening for her eyes to peer out. She snuck out of her home and merged with the throng of people trying to catch a glimpse of the much-acclaimed healer and teacher. Gathering all the courage she could muster, she pushed her way through the crowd in hopes of getting close enough just to touch the hem of His robe.

"Jesus!" a man called from the crowd. Like the parting of the sea, the multitude gave way for the synagogue ruler to pass. Everyone knew Jairus. He was important.

Jesus turned as Jairus fell at his feet and begged. "My little daughter is dying," he began. "Please come and put Your hands on her so that she will be healed and live."

The woman looked on as Jesus extended His hand to this distraught father, compassionately helped him to his feet, and apparently changed course to go with him. It was then she made her move.

Shoring up all the courage she could muster, Lydia began muttering to herself. "If I can but touch His clothes, I will be healed. I know it. I just know it. I can't let this opportunity slip away." While unsure of herself, she was confident in Him. Her faith overcame her fear, and she pressed forward.

Like a runner stretching for the finish line, the woman reached through the crowd and brushed her fingers against the hem of His garment. Just as her faith reached out to touch Jesus, God's healing power reached down to touch her. Immediately, she felt a surge of power flow through her body and the flow of blood come to a halt.

She knew it. She felt it. The flow stopped…and then Jesus stopped.

"Who just touched My robe?" He asked.

The woman kept her eyes fixed to the ground as a jumble of thoughts scrambled through her mind. *I'm unclean and not supposed to be out in public. I'm not supposed to touch anyone. What am I going to do? If I remove my veil people will recognize me.* She wanted to run, but it was as though her feet were suddenly rooted to the ground.

"Many people are crowding against You," His disciples answered. "Why do you ask, 'Who touched Me'?"

Jesus ignored His disciples and continued to scan the crowd in search of the person who had purposely touched His robe. He had felt the power flow from His body like a current. He knew what had happened. Jesus could always sense the difference between the press of the curious and the touch of the faithful.

Silence hung like a low-lying cloud. No one said a word.

Finally, she couldn't hold it in any longer. She turned to Jesus and fell at His feet. With trembling voice, a geyser of gratitude and confession gushed forth.

"Master, I have had an issue of blood for more than 12 years. I have gone from doctor to doctor, and no one has been able to help me. I've lost my family, my friends, and my finances. But when I heard that You were passing through, I just knew that You, Lord, could heal me. I know I'm not supposed to touch anyone. I know that I am unclean in all regards. Please forgive me for the intrusion. But, Jesus, what I have to tell You is this! I am healed! As soon as I touched the hem of Your robe, the blood ceased to flow! Thank You, Jesus. Thank You, Jesus."

While others began to back away from her "uncleanness," Jesus reached forward to confirm her wholeness. "Daughter, your faith has healed you. Go in peace and be freed from your suffering."

A Closer Look

Oh, how I love this story! What woman among us hasn't felt the wretchedness of rejection, the shame of suffering, and the humility of hopelessness? What woman hasn't wondered, *Would God care about the likes of me?* And here we have a story of just how much God values and esteems His female image bearers. He singles out one lone woman from a multitude of curious followers, heals her of her affliction with but a touch, and then shines the heavenly spotlight center stage for her to testify of the miraculous transformation. Let's take a closer look.

> *When Jesus had again crossed over by boat to the other side of the lake, a large crowd gathered around him while he was by the lake. Then one of the synagogue rulers, named Jairus came there. Seeing Jesus, he fell at his feet and pleaded earnestly with him. "My little daughter is dying. Please come and put your hands on her so that she will be healed and live." So Jesus went with him. A large crowd followed and pressed around him. And a woman was there who had been subject to bleeding for twelve years. She had suffered a great deal under the care of many doctors and had spent all she had, yet instead of getting better she grew worse (Mark 5:21-26).*

The woman we meet in Mark 5 has been called "the woman with the issue of blood." She was defined by what was wrong with her. I've given her the name Lydia to help us remember that she was a real person, not just an insignificant character in a story.

For 12 long years, this woman had been bleeding; we can assume it was vaginally. When we meet her, she is physically, financially, socially, and spiritually drained—bankrupt in every way.

In biblical days, certain situations and conditions rendered a person ceremonially unclean. Leprous people were separated from society and had to shout, "Unclean! Unclean!" when they walked among common folk. Anyone who touched a dead body was considered unclean. And a woman was considered unclean during her monthly period.

For seven days, considered the time of a normal female period, a woman was secluded. A woman hemorrhaging for 12 years would be considered permanently unclean. If unmarried, she would not be able to marry. If married, her condition would be grounds for divorce. She would be expelled from her home, cut off from her family, and ostracized by her community.

Each doctor's visit brought a surge of hope and expectation, only to be swept away when the red flow of despair reappeared. The joy of tender youth was now a vague memory, crushed by life's hardness and the weight of disappointment. The hammer of rejection drove the nails of isolation into the coffin of her tightly secured heart.

Unlike the lame man who was lowered through the roof by four friends and placed at Jesus' feet, this woman apparently had no one to intercede for her. There was no father pleading for his daughter. There was no husband praying for his wife. There was no master imploring Jesus' help to heal a servant. When we meet this woman, she is fearful and forgotten. She is all alone—or so it seemed to her.

Sometimes we can feel the same. Abandoned by friends. Deserted by a spouse. Forgotten by family. Unseen by society. But she was not forgotten. She was not alone. This daughter of Abraham was close to God's heart and foremost on His mind. So God the Father orchestrated His Son's journey to pass her way.

> *When she heard about Jesus, she came up behind him in the crowd and touched his cloak, because she thought, "If I just touch his clothes, I will be healed" (Mark 5:27-28).*

This woman understood that Jesus was radically different in His approach and appreciation of women. "Apparently, this was a man who was willing to disrupt the status quo by delivering people from cruel diseases and evil oppression. He was willing to risk making enemies by liberating women from centuries of repression and pious tradition. She would take advantage of His kindness."[1]

She knew full well that she was overstepping cultural and religious boundaries set out by pious men of her day, but it was a risk she was willing to take.

> *Immediately her bleeding stopped and she felt in her body that*
> *she was freed from her suffering. At once Jesus realized that*
> *power had gone out from him. He turned around in the crowd*
> *and asked, "Who touched my clothes?" (Mark 5:29-30).*

Two things happened when the woman touched Jesus. First, she was healed. It was measurable. She felt the ceasing of the flow of blood. Jesus felt the releasing of the power of God.

Second, she was revealed. Her courage, cloaked in anonymity, trembled in the fear of exposure, but Jesus was not going to allow her to steal her healing. He wanted to do more than stop the flow of blood. He wanted to start the flow of ministry. He called her forward to testify, to tell what had just happened to her so that others would believe.

> *"You see the people crowding against you," his disciples*
> *answered, "and yet you can ask, 'Who touched me?'" But*
> *Jesus kept looking around to see who had done it. Then the*
> *woman, knowing what had happened to her, came and fell*
> *at his feet and, trembling with fear, told him the whole truth.*
> *He said to her, "Daughter, your faith has healed you. Go in*
> *peace and be freed from your suffering" (Mark 5:31-34).*

A rabbi did not speak to a woman in public, but once again, Jesus, the Liberator, broke the man-made rules for a God-made woman. He did not call her out to embarrass or shame her in any way. He wanted to honor her honesty, to commend her courage, and to validate her valor. He did not reprimand her for breaking the religious rules but praised her great faith.

Once again, Jesus called a woman from out of the shadows and placed her center stage. No longer was she a woman in need of a healing touch, but now a believer who had received it and was called on to tell about it. He placed a woman on equal standing with men and addressed her in public, called her to testify, and sent her away healthy and spiritually whole. He publically affirmed her as a person, and confirmed her as a child of God.

"*Daughter,* your faith has healed you." Can we just stop there for a moment? Sometimes one single word in Scripture speaks volumes. Why did Jesus call her "Daughter"? It seems to me that while Jairus was concerned for his daughter, God was also concerned for His. She is and would always be a child of God. And while all other family members may have deserted her in her affliction, God, her heavenly Father, had drawn near. "Daughter" was a term of endearment she would not easily forget.

When Jesus said the word "healed," it is the Greek word *sesoken,* which means "saved." Jesus did more than heal her body. He saved her soul, removed her shame, and reestablished her place in the community. As with this particular woman and the others we will visit, Jesus viewed their needs as portals through which deeper spiritual needs might be met. His miraculous healings were the chain cutters that set women free from physical, emotional, and spiritual disease to physical, emotional, and spiritual health. He ministered to their immediate needs and gave them an eternal perspective and great significance.

We can't leave this scene quite yet. If you recall, Jesus was on His way somewhere else when the woman reached out to grab hold of her healing.

> *One of the synagogue rulers, named Jairus, came there...*
> *"My little daughter is dying. Please come and put your hands*
> *on her so that she will be healed and live." So Jesus went with*
> *him (Mark 5:22-24).*

Mingled together like two skeins of yarn, the story of the bleeding woman is knitted together with Jairus' dying 12-year-old daughter. We can't miss the time frame. The woman had suffered for 12 years. The girl had lived 12 years. The woman had a chronic illness. The child had an acute sickness.

Jairus was a big shot in this local Jewish community, but the thought of losing a child made him see the truth that he was indeed very small. He might have had power in the synagogue, but he was powerless to save his little princess.

Not many religious leaders in Jesus' day openly professed a belief that He was the Messiah. I've often heard the saying: "There are no atheists in foxholes." When under heavy fire and enemy attack, when the guns of adversity are blazing overhead, even the hardest heart will cry out, "God help me! God save me!"

Perhaps that is what we see in Jairus. "My little daughter is dying," he cried. "Please come and put Your hands on her so that she will be healed and live." Jesus didn't condemn him for his sudden belief. "Oh, right. *Now* you believe in Me. When you want something, you come running." We never see Jesus with that attitude. He simply changed His course and went with Jairus to work a miracle in his life. Don't you just love Him!

Have you ever wondered what was going through Jairus' mind as Jesus stopped to take care of the woman who touched His robe? *Wait a minute, I was here first,* he might have thought. *My daughter is more important. Let's get this show on the road.*

Aren't you glad that Jesus has enough grace for everyone? He's not going to run out of blessings. He had enough healing power for the desperate woman and the dying girl…and He has all the time in the world.

> While Jesus was still speaking, some men came from the house of Jairus, the synagogue ruler. "Your daughter is dead," they said. "Why bother the teacher any more?" Ignoring what they said, Jesus told the synagogue ruler, "Don't be afraid; just believe." He did not let anyone follow him except Peter, James and John the brother of James. When they came to the home of the synagogue ruler, Jesus saw a commotion, with people crying and wailing loudly. He went in and said to them, "Why all this commotion and wailing? The child is not dead but asleep." But they laughed at him (Mark 5:35-40).

"They laughed at him." Hmm. When was the last time you inwardly laughed when someone told you not to give up hope? When was the last time you silently chuckled when someone told you, "Just believe"? When was the last time you sighed when someone reminded you that God was a God of miracles?

Well, the joke was on them.

> *After he put them out, he took the child's father and mother and the disciples who were with him, and went in where the child was. He took her by the hand and said to her, "Talitha koum!" (which means, "Little girl, I say to you, get up!"). Immediately the girl stood up and walked around (she was twelve years old). At this they were completely astonished (Mark 5:40-42).*

Here is something I want you to notice: Jesus was so intentional. God was so precise. This was a culture that cared very little for women, much less a little girl. But here comes Jesus, breaking cultural rules and societal norms to heal, embrace, and set free God's female image bearers. He interrupts the course of His day to attend to a little 12-year-old girl. He stops midstream to minister to a lone woman. They were both important to Jesus. They were both important to God.

What sort of God would do that? A God who loves, cherishes, and highly esteems His grand finale of creation—woman. This, my friend, was radical. A splash of cold water in the face of societal prejudice, discrimination, and unmitigated segregation.

As Augustine wrote: "God loves each of us as if there were only one of us to love."[2] He's crazy about you.

Freed from Hopelessness

For us in the twenty-first century, it is hard to imagine bleeding from the womb for 12 years. Medical science has progressed way beyond the rudimentary knowledge of Jesus' day.

But I suggest there are still many women with chronic bleeding of a different sort. We bleed from the heart.

From the time Sarah was six years old, her father crept into her bedroom in the dark of night and violated her little body. Now, as an adult, her heart bleeds.

When Beth was walking to her dorm room from the college library, a lurker jumped from behind the bushes, dragged her to a nearby shed, and raped her at knifepoint. Now, ten years later, her heart bleeds.

After 20 years of marriage, Lucy accidentally stumbled upon a hotel receipt in her husband's wallet. Suspecting the worst, she uncovered past e-mails, supposed meetings that never occurred, and a trail of deceit. When presented with the evidence, her husband admitted having a three-year long affair. And her heart bleeds.

Margaret's routine physical reveals that she has AIDS. She had only been with one man her entire life…her husband. And her heart bleeds.

Laura was laid off from her job, and her mother's words reemerge like sewage leakage from an underground septic tank. "You're no good. You'll never amount to anything. You're a loser just like your father." And because of the lies, her heart bleeds.

Melissa holds her newborn little girl in her arms and coos her to sleep. Interrupting the sweetness of the wee hours of the morning, she hears her aborted child crying from the grave. Guilt presses down as the ever-present weight deflates her joy. And her heart bleeds.

Women—hoping the pain will go away. Awakening each day with a memory that cuts a fresh wound. Women—longing to hear the words "Go in peace and be freed from your suffering."

The woman with the issue of blood was no different from you and me. While her apparent illness was physical, her inward suffering ruled her life. But in one radical moment, one momentous decision, she reached out to Jesus and grabbed hold of her healing.

Mark used specific words to describe our friend with the issue of blood. She "suffered a great deal." Jesus used the word "suffer" when He was referring to His last days on earth (Mark 8:31; 9:12). Jesus understood her suffering more than she knew. As the blood flowed from her body and rendered her unclean, Jesus knew the blood that would soon flow from His body would cleanse us all.

Jesus wants to set us free from our suffering, but He will not push us out of our prison. He unlocks the jail cell, but we must walk out the door. We can choose to bleed. We can choose to remain in our suffering and pick at the scabs of the past. But hear me, dear friend. It is a choice. Jesus said, "I have come that they might have life and have it to the full" (John 10:10). That's what He wants for each of us. But we have to embrace the truth and reach for our healing.

In John 5, Jesus encounters a lame man sitting by a pool of water where the paralyzed, blind, and afflicted gathered. They believed that when the waters stirred, supposedly by angels, the first one in the pool would be healed. For 38 years this man sat in his sickness.

Then Jesus walked up to him and asked a strange question. "Do you want to get well?" (John 5:6).

Perhaps it was not such a strange question after all. Many times we get used to being sick and wear our pain like a shroud. Emotionally we are the walking wounded—victims who pick at scabs, not allowing them to heal.

Jesus said to the woman, "Daughter, your faith has healed you. Go in peace and be freed from your suffering" (Mark 5:34). That is the same healing He offers to you and to me.

Freed to Share the Hope Within Her

Jesus could have easily let this woman slip away with her healing, but He would have none of that. He wanted her to tell the crowd what had happened. So He called her center stage and waited for her to take her place.

"It was me," she finally cried. And then she broke the rules. She testified about what had happened to her before the anxious crowd. Luke adds an interesting sentence in his account of this story. "Then the woman, seeing that she could not go unnoticed, came trembling and fell at his feet. *In the presence of all the people,* she told why she had touched him and how she had been instantly healed" (Luke 8:47).

In the presence of all the people. Remember, this was a time in history when women were considered to be unreliable, and a woman's testimony was inadmissible and unacceptable as evidence in a court of law.

But Jesus debunked their way of thinking. She was a key witness to the power of God working through His Son. There was no way He was going to let her slip away with her healing. He had work for her to do. She now had a story to tell. And tell it she must!

Once again, Jesus took a woman who had previously moved about in the shadows of society and called her center stage. She came to Jesus in secret but left telling everyone what He had done.

She was free *from* her suffering.

She was now free *to* tell about it.

> *The women who proclaim the good tidings are a great host.*
>
> PSALM 68:11 NASB

5

THE ASHAMED ADULTERESS

Freed from Condemnation
Freed to Start Anew

What are we going to do with this Jesus?" the chief priest asked the group. "He is going about healing people left and right. Everywhere I go the buzz is about Him. It's Jesus this, Jesus that. And the crowds are calling Him the Messiah! Everyone knows that the Messiah will not come from Galilee. If we don't get rid of Him, we are going to have an insurrection on our hands.

"And ever since the buzz about Him multiplying a few loaves and fish to feed more than 5000 people has circulated, His followers have multiplied as well," another priest added. "He must be stopped."

"I have an idea," Lucius responded with a gleam in his eye. "I happen to know a certain married man who is sleeping with his mistress at this very moment. I saw him slink into her house last night."

And as the hard-hearted Pharisees gathered round, a spiteful plan to trick Jesus began to unfold.

The sun was just peeking through the securely locked shutters of Morah's bedroom window. The early morning stillness was broken only by birdsong floating on the breeze. Morah was a tangle of sheets, arms, and legs as the man she loved lay sleeping beside her.

"Oh, Zachariah," she whispered as her fingertips brushed a stray lock of hair from his closed eyes. "If only you weren't married. I know this is wrong, but I love you so. And I have to believe you when you say you love me as well. We are risking our very lives with these frequent trysts."

Morah's musings were suddenly interrupted by a banging on the door.

"Open up!" the gruff voice demanded.

"Who is there?" Morah cried.

"Open up or we'll break the door down."

"What's all the commotion," Zachariah mumbled as he groggily sat up in bed. "What's going on?"

Before Morah could even think to answer, an angry mob of religious men broke through the simple lock and into the lovers' hideaway.

"What is the meaning of this?" Zachariah barked. "What do you think you are doing?"

"What do you think *you* are doing, my friend?" the Pharisee countered. "That is the real question here."

"Morah daughter of Omar, you are under arrest for adultery under the law of Moses!" the moral police spat. "Get dressed and come with me."

The Pharisee tossed Morah her night robe, but he failed to turn his head as she slipped her trembling frame from the cover of the sheets and into the thin garment. He grabbed her by the arm and began dragging her to the door.

"Where are you taking me?" she cried.

"You'll find out soon enough," the Pharisee growled.

"What about Zachariah?" the youngest man of the group inquired.

"Just leave him. We don't need him."

"Wait!" Zechariah called. But already he could see that protesting was no use.

"Why don't you go back to your wife where you belong," the Pharisee called over his shoulder as the group left the room. And with that, the conspiring mob continued their trek to the temple with the half-clad, trembling woman in tow. Two men flanked her on either side, dragging her through the early morning hustle and bustle of the city. The bait was hooked, and now it was time to reel in the catch.

Like mice following the Pied Piper, a curious stream of townsfolk joined the parade. Jesus was already teaching in the courtyard with a group gathered around Him. As always, Jesus' message and miracles drew large crowds. A distant rumble interrupted His words as the angry mob and curious crowd approached. They marched right into the inner circle of the classroom and thrust the woman at the Master's feet.

Morah's unbound hair fell around her bare shoulders and fluttered in the early morning breeze. Her shame-filled eyes stayed riveted on the earthen floor, refusing to meet Jesus' gaze. Then one of the men pulled her to her feet and displayed her for all to see.

"Teacher," the pious Pharisee began, "we caught this woman in the act of adultery. The law of Moses says she should be stoned. What do You say?"

Jesus didn't look at the woman's half-clad body as the others openly gawked. He looked into her soul.

Morah lifted her eyes and looked into the face of love. *What do I detect in His gaze?* she thought to herself. It wasn't contempt, disgust, or condemnation, but rather compassion, concern, and pure unadulterated affection. Somehow she knew this was the look she had been searching for her entire life.

As she listened to the Pharisee's question, she understood Jesus' dilemma. If He set her free, the Pharisees would accuse Him of ignoring the law of Moses and deem Him a heretic. If He sentenced her to death by stoning, then His teachings of grace and forgiveness would be negated.

The religious leaders already held stones in their clenched fists, anticipating Jesus' reply. Their hearts were as hard as the rocks in their hands. But rather than giving a quick answer, Jesus moved His gaze from the trembling woman and stooped to the ground. With His finger, the very hand of God-made-man, He began writing in the dirt. A frigid chill swept through the Pharisees' pious robes. Suddenly they felt the rawness of naked exposure as Jesus' eyes looked up at each of them and without a word, uncloaked their sinful thoughts and desires. With one look from Jesus, they stood soul bare and more exposed than the half-dressed woman before them.

Everyone held their breath. The silence was deafening. The tension was palpable. Finally, Jesus rose and delivered the verdict.

"If any one of you is without sin, let him be the first to throw a stone at her."

Then He squatted once again and continued to write.

One by one the Pharisees unclenched their fists, dropped their stones, and filtered through the crowd. The older men who had accumulated a longer list of sins turned to leave first, with the younger ones not far behind.

The remaining crowd listened closely as the drama continued to unfold. After the last of the Pharisees cleared the scene, Jesus straightened up and asked her, "Woman, what happened to your accusers? Does no one remain to condemn you?"

"No one, sir," she replied.

"Then neither do I," Jesus declared. "Go now and do not repeat your sin."

The woman turned to leave, but not before picking up a discarded stone to take with her.

"To remember," she whispered.

A Closer Look

Jesus' ministry and miracles caused quite a stir everywhere He put His sandaled foot. His authoritative teaching to the masses, passionate clearing out of the temple courts, and confusing prophecy of the destruction and resurrection of the temple made people sit up and take notice.[1] Jesus expanded His ministry to include the Samaritans (led by the first woman evangelist) and then back to Galilee, where He healed a royal official's son, commanded a lame man to take up his pallet and walk, and fed 5000 men plus women and

children with no more than five loaves and two fish.[2] The multitudes wanted to make Jesus king. The scribes and Pharisees wanted
to make Jesus disappear.

Jesus knew the Jewish religious leaders wanted to kill him, yet He
continued ministering publically and prophetically. They looked for
reasons to discredit and accuse Him. So they came up with a plan to
trick Him and publicly humiliate Him before His followers. Let's
take a closer look at how they used a woman as bait but were snared
by their own trap.

Jesus went to the Mount of Olives (John 8:1).

The night before this incident, Jesus had been on the Mount of
Olives praying. The mount is directly east of Jerusalem and rises
about 2700 feet. This summit offered a magnificent view of the city
and the temple below. How appropriate that Jesus would spend His
time alone with God while looking down at the apple of His eye.

> *At dawn he appeared again in the temple courts, where all*
> *the people gathered around him, and he sat down to teach*
> *them (John 8:2).*

Early the next morning, He came to the temple to teach. John
tells us "all the people" gather around Him. When I see "all," I think
all. The radical Rabbi teaching both men and women.

> *The teachers of the law and the Pharisees brought in a*
> *woman caught in adultery (John 8:3).*

The Sanhedrin, or religious leaders, forced their way into the center of those gathered around Jesus, and interrupted His teaching. I
suspect this was no interruption to Jesus at all. I suspect He was expecting them all along.

They could have kept the woman in custody and brought the
accusation before Jesus rather than bringing the accused, but they
were not concerned with her public humiliation. They thrived on it.

The fact that she was "caught in the act" smells of a setup. It could have been that they planned the tryst by planting an enticing cohort to seduce her. Or it could have been that the relationship was common knowledge and everyone had turned a blind eye before. There were no video cameras or private investigators with revealing photos back then, so when they say "caught in the act," that means they walked in on the scene. Whatever the case, the men paraded their catch of the day through the city streets for all to see.

"As Nathaniel Hawthorne wrote of Hester Prynne's morning journey from the darkness of her jail cell to the unforgiving light of day, 'Iniquity is dragged out into the sunshine. Come along, Madam Hester, and show your scarlet letter in the marketplace.'"[3] And just as Hester Prynne's partner in the tryst remained conspicuously absent from the public eye, the woman caught in adultery stood conspicuously alone.

I doubt these men gave the accused time to get fully clothed or pin her hair back in place. The idea of a woman walking through the streets with her hair unbound was scandalous in itself, much less being half dressed and manhandled by angry pious priests.

> *They made her stand before the group and said to Jesus,*
> *"Teacher, this woman was caught in the act of adultery" (John*
> *8:3-4).*

The Pharisees were considered the "custodians of public morality."[4] They were supposed to be the good guys, but in reality they were quite the opposite. How does that happen? It happens when religion and law replace relationship and love—things get ugly.

There was no denying the accusation. Apparently they had walked right in on her and her lover. Apparently they knew where to go to find such an incident taking place. The woman was no more than a pawn in their plan and a tool in their treachery. So they cast the bait...

> *"In the Law Moses commanded us to stone such women"*
> *(John 8:5).*

Ah, excuse me, boys, but there is someone missing here. Last time I checked, it takes two to commit adultery. As for the law, let's take a look at what it really said:

> If a man commits adultery with another man's wife—with the wife of his neighbor—both the adulterer and the adulteress must be put to death (Leviticus 20:10).

> If a man is found sleeping with another man's wife, both the man who slept with her and the woman must die. You must purge the evil from Israel (Deuteronomy 22:22).

While we do not know if this woman was another man's wife, it was not the first time, and would not be the last, that a woman was left to carry the consequences of sexual sin alone. Jesus didn't address this little detail, most likely because He knew that seeking justice was not the purpose of the Pharisees' visit in the first place. They couldn't have cared less about the immorality issue standing before them. If they were truly interested in keeping the moral law of Moses, then both partners would have been standing before them. Their only concern was setting a trap for Jesus.

> *"Now, what do you say?" They were using this question as a trap, in order to have a basis for accusing him (John 8:5).*

To those looking on, it might appear that Jesus was caught between a rock and a hard place. But what they didn't realize is that Jesus IS the rock; there is no hard place He can't push aside.

> *But Jesus bent down and started to write on the ground with his finger (John 8:6).*

I'm sure it threw them off a bit when Jesus stooped to write in the dirt. This is the only time that Scripture records Jesus writing anything. Could it be that He was trying to distract the people's attention away from the half-dressed woman and onto Himself? It sounds just like something my Jesus would do.

What did Jesus write? Nobody knows for sure. Some commentaries suggest He scribbled down the sins of the Pharisees. Some suggest He was doodling to present a pregnant pause, giving the accusers time to think. "There is often a power in holy silence that no words, however eloquent, can carry."⁵ What He wrote is not important, but what He said was powerful.

> *When they kept on questioning him, he straightened up and said to them, "If any one of you is without sin, let him be the first to throw a stone at her" (John 8:7).*

What an answer! Jesus uncovered their own hearts and left them exposed and spiritually naked before the crowd. Now who was stuck between a rock and a hard place? Each man standing knew his own life was riddled with sin. The prophet Isaiah, whose writings they knew very well, wrote: "We all, like sheep have gone astray, each of us has turned to his own way" (Isaiah 53:6). To throw a stone and thus imply that he was without sin would have been the greatest heresy of the entire scenario.

Isn't it interesting that the only person qualified to throw a stone at the woman is the One who set her free?

> *Again he stooped down and wrote on the ground (John 8:8).*

Sometimes the shortest answers are the most powerful. Jesus gave His answer and then let them think on it. No hurry. Just chew on that for a while. I think it would be a good time for us to chew on it ourselves. If I were sitting right there with you, I'd want us to chat about what "Let him who is without sin throw the first stone" means in our own lives. It is easy to smirk at those self-righteous, pious Pharisees and say, "Hah! Take that!" But what about you and me? When is the last time you threw a stone at someone? Maybe not a real stone, but a stone-hard, judgmental attitude tossed someone's way?

> *At this, those who heard began to go away one at a time, the older ones first... (John 8:9).*

Jesus took the mirror of condemnation and flipped it around for the men to get a good look at their own lives. What they saw was not pretty. One by one they began to leave.

The woman was brought to Jesus in shame, but she received grace and forgiveness. The accusers came to Jesus in self-righteous piety, but they skulked away condemned. The older ones with the much longer list of sins were the first to turn and slink away. I tell you the truth, the older I get, the more merciful toward others I become. In my early adult years, I was much quicker to pass judgment on others. But the longer I've lived, the more mistakes I've made, and the more clearly God has revealed my own shortcomings and failures. As John Bradford said when a drunk was led through town to be placed in the public stocks, "But by the grace of God, there go I."

> *...until only Jesus was left, with the woman still standing there (John 8:9).*

Many commentaries noted that Jesus and the woman were left alone. However, before the confrontation began, Jesus was teaching "all" who came to the temple to hear Him. There is no indication that those people left. It could be that only the accusers slipped away. I imagine the onlookers were glued to their seats watching the drama unfold. I know I would have been.

But as Jesus so often does, He sees through the crowd and zooms in on one particular lamb that needs His sole attention. At the end of the day, that is all that matters for any of us. It doesn't matter what anyone else thinks of us. Only Jesus' opinion matters.

> *Jesus straightened up and asked her, "Woman, where are they? Has no one condemned you?" (John 8:10).*

While the Pharisees spoke *about* her with disdain, Jesus spoke *to* her with respect. Never do we see Jesus speaking disrespectfully or turning His back on God's female image bearers who crossed His path. This is the same way He addressed His mother at the wedding of Cana and again at the foot of the cross. It can be translated "Dear woman."

The woman caught in adultery stood before the Son of God—and disgrace was met with divine grace, embarrassment with envelopment, cruelty with caring, disregard with high regard. That's my Jesus.

As He often does, Jesus asked her a question to help her come to her own conclusion. His question-asking was a pattern we see all through the New Testament. "Which is easier: to say to the paralytic, 'Your sins are forgiven,' or to say, 'Get up, take your mat and walk'?" (Mark 2:9). "Do you want to get well?" (John 5:6). "Which is lawful on the Sabbath: to do good or to do evil, to save life or to kill?" (Mark 3:4). "Do you bring a lamp and put it under a bowl?" (Mark 4:21). "Who do people say that I am…But what about you…Who do you say that I am?" (Mark 8:27,29).

Jesus is omniscient; He knows the answers. He didn't ask questions to gather information. Instead, He used questions to get people to think, and many times to help them come to right conclusions.

"Woman, where are they? Has no one condemned you?" Another translation says, "Woman, where are your accusers?" (John 8:10 AMP). Jesus turned the accusers into the accused. That is always the risk we take when we start pointing fingers—in that balled up fist of ours, there are usually three fingers pointing right back at our own hearts.

"No one, sir," she said (John 8:11).

Imagine yourself, standing before God on your day of judgment. You know all that you have done. Satan is pacing back and forth, reading your long list of sins. But then Jesus steps forward and takes the list from the accuser. Looking over the list, He begins: "I paid for this one, and this one, and this one, and this one…"

Finally, reaching the end of Satan's meticulously penned and amazingly accurate enumeration of all your shortcomings, Jesus begins to tear the paper into shreds. He cups the pieces of the destroyed list of failures in His nail-scarred hands and then, with the breath of grace, blows them as far as the east is from the west. Wiping His hands together as if completing a work, He glances back over to the Judge. "All gone," He says with a smile.

Satan grumbles under his sulfurous breath, and slinks back to his darkened cave—foiled again.

God looks up and asks you, "Has no one condemned you?"

"No one, sir," you reply.

"Then enter My eternal kingdom and find rest."

Friend, if you have accepted Jesus as your Lord and Savior, and if you are still feeling *condemned*, know that condemnation is not coming from God. Our enemy, the devil or Satan, is called the "accuser of the brothers," and he is the accuser of the sisters as well. The Bible tells us that he "accuses them before our God day and night" (Revelation 12:10). All day long he marches back and forth, accusing the believers. "She did this and that and that and this." And God replies, "Really? I don't remember."

However, if you are feeling *convicted* today, that is another story. The Holy Spirit convicts us of sin in order to get us to turn from sin and go in the opposite direction. See, that is what Jesus did with this woman. He did not condemn her. He convicted her and told her to turn and go in the opposite direction.

Condemnation says, "You are bad."

Conviction says, "What you did was bad."

Jesus called sin a sin, but then He told her to leave that destructive lifestyle and start anew.

> *"Then neither do I condemn you," Jesus declared. "Go now and leave your life of sin" (John 8:11).*

Freed from Condemnation

Jesus came to set the prisoners free. And even though the woman caught in adultery was not behind metal bars, she was in bondage to a sinful lifestyle. Sexual sin is highly addictive, and the search for love in all the wrong places is often insatiable. It is a drink that never satisfies the soul and leaves the partaker only thirsty for more.

What was the adulteress thinking? This was a day when a woman caught in adultery could be stoned to death? Was it worth it? No. The answer is always no.

Sex outside of marriage can lead to many things: unwanted pregnancy, sexually transmitted diseases, divorce, mistrust, regret, shame, loss of family, and a whole list of undesirable dominos that tumble in succession. But in Jesus' day, a woman caught in the act of adultery faced possible execution. (Even today, in some parts of the world adultery is punishable by death.) So why would she take the risk? Love. The desire to love and be loved can sometimes override the wisdom of reason.

There is no greater longing in the heart of a woman than to be loved, cherished, and cared for. It can cause the strongest to break a resolve and succumb to the tempter's lure. Adultery has been the cause for church leaders to crumble, ministries to melt down, families to falter. Sexual sin has caused the sensible to act like a fool, the moral to march into madness, the devout to be devoured by desire. The yearning for love gnarls at the heart. And then the brush of a hand, the catch of the eyes, the stirring of a comment. Loneliness echoes in the hollow soul just as passion comes scratching at the door.

God designed our hearts to desire love because He longs for us to have that longing filled by a relationship with Him. Unfortunately, many settle for a sip from the rusty tin cup when God offers an everlasting stream.

A woman can risk it all for a few moments of passion. She can lie to herself that it is love. Then, after the brief pleasure lies exposed by the morning sun, she realizes that what felt like love was tainted with the poison of shame. It can happen. It does happen. It happened to this friend standing before Jesus with an angry mob of rock-holding Pharisees gathered round.

So what now?

Jesus.

Jesus was not surprised by the Pharisees' interruption. After all, He had spent the night in prayer with His heavenly Father. The Pharisees might have thought they were interrupting Jesus' teaching and catching Him off guard, but in reality they were bringing forth an object lesson of grace.

Here's what John wrote about God's grace demonstrated through Jesus Christ:

God so loved the world that he gave his one and only Son, that whoever believes in him shall not perish but have eternal life. For God did not send his Son into the world to condemn the world, but to save the world through him. Whoever believes in him is not condemned, but whoever does not believe stands condemned already because he has not believed in the name of God's one and only Son (John 3:16-18).

Paul later wrote of Jesus' finished work on the cross:

There is now no condemnation for those who are in Christ Jesus (Romans 8:1).

None?
None.

We do not read of this woman's verbal statement of faith, but Jesus knew what was in her heart. He knew she was repentant, and He freed her *from* condemnation and freed her *to* start anew. The religious leaders put her down like dirt. Jesus looked at her with compassion and lifted her out of it. How refreshing it must have been to meet a man who was not interested in exploiting her, but freeing her.

Laura was a girl much like the woman in this story. Living in a small town, she grew up with parents who were morally sound. She went to church from her earliest remembrance and was baptized when she was 12 years old. In high school she began dating Barry. After Laura went off to college, both of Barry's parents died. He was lonely and missed the close-knit family he had once enjoyed.

After Laura's first year of college, Barry began talking marriage. He had not gone to college and wanted her to come home and be his wife. Laura was torn, but she made the decision to marry Barry and continue working toward her degree.

Laura and I held hands and prayed together before she walked down the aisle. It was a beautiful day as I stood with her and the two were united as man and wife. But after the wedding comes the marriage—something that neither 19-year-old Laura nor Barry were prepared to face.

After five years, Laura was bored with the marriage, restless in her job, and disappointed in her husband. While working in a medical office, Bob, a salesman for an international medical supply company, took on their account. Bob was older and lived what seemed like an exciting lifestyle. Friendly bantering progressed to enticing flirtation. Laura found herself looking forward to Thursdays—the day Bob made his weekly visits.

A touch here, a lunch there, and soon an affair ensued. Laura packed her bags, left her marriage, her job, and her hometown to move to greener pastures. But the greener pastures weren't so green. Thorns infested the relationship. Bob wasn't interested in anything long term. Laura was just a young plaything he toyed with on weekends. What promised to be an exciting life away from small-town America, away from a mundane and monotonous marriage, turned into a deep, dark pit of regret and remorse. Laura discovered Bob wasn't anything special. He was just someone different. A diversion. She was his flavor of the month.

After her divorce was final, Laura was left all alone in a strange town. "What have I done?" she cried.

Laura's husband remarried and put the broken pieces of his life back together. Laura, on the other hand, was just broken.

I gathered up my friend and brought her to my hometown. My husband and I found her a job, helped her get her finances in order, and directed her to a great Bible-based church. That's what it looked like on the outside, but here's what really happened.

Laura, in her own world, stood before Jesus like the woman caught in adultery. She felt the stares of her accusers and recoiled in anticipation of the rocks that would surely fly. In her own mind, she stood naked and ashamed before her community, her childhood church body, and her lifelong friends. But more important, she stood in shame before Jesus.

"I didn't think God would forgive me," she began. "I had hurt my family, my husband, and my witness. What would God want with someone like me?"

"Laura," I said, "we are all sinners. We are all saved by grace. None of us deserves it. That's what makes grace, grace. You made a terrible mistake. But so did the woman the Pharisees brought to Jesus who had been caught in adultery. What did Jesus do with that woman? What did He say?"

"He told her to go and sin no more."

"Exactly. He told her to leave her life of sin. That doesn't mean she never sinned again, but we can safely believe that she left this lifestyle, this sinful relationship, and began a new life. That is what Jesus will do for you. That is what He does for all of us."

First John 1:9 promises: "If we confess our sins, he is faithful and just and will forgive us our sins and purify us from all unrighteousness." Another translation uses the words "cleanse us from all unrighteousness" (NASB). I love the picture of God washing away all our sins, erasing the list of offenses, throwing our sins into the deepest of seas. All gone.

Laura did begin again. She repented of her sin, immersed herself in Bible study and ministry, and began a new life totally committed to the One who forgave her and set her free from condemnation. And that, my friend, is what Jesus does for each and every one of us who comes to Him with a repentant heart ready to start anew.

Freed to Start Anew

"Go now and leave your life of sin," Jesus declared (John 8:11). That is the very definition of repentance—to turn and go in the opposite direction. Let's be very clear. Jesus did not say that what the woman did was okay. He called sin a sin. And yet He gave her the open door to start anew. He gave her the freedom to start over with a clean slate.

This sort of grace bothers a lot of folks. It certainly bothered the prodigal son's brother. In Luke 15 is the story of a young man who took his inheritance before his father even died. Then he proceeded to squander his wealth in wild living—drinking, gambling, prostitutes, you name it. But when his pockets and stomach were empty, when "he began to be in need" and "came to his senses" (Luke 15:14,17), he returned home in hopes of working as a farmhand.

> But while he was still a long way off, his father saw him and was filled with compassion for him; he ran to his son, threw his arms around him and kissed him. The son said to him, "Father, I have sinned against heaven and against you. I am no longer worthy to be called your son." But the father said to his servants, "Quick! Bring the best robe and put it on him. Put a ring on his finger and sandals on his feet. Bring the fattened calf and kill it. Let's have a feast and celebrate. For this son of mine was dead and is alive again; he was lost and is found." So they began to celebrate (Luke 15:20-24).

Don't you love it! Jesus is telling this story. He is trying to make a point. When a repentant sinner comes home to the Father, that man or woman is not met with condemnation. He or she is not met with rock-throwing religious folk ready to pass judgment and sentence the wayward to death. No, a repentant sinner is met by a loving Father who has been waiting...panning the horizon...for His child to come home.

Then, of all things, God throws a party! The repentant child gets to throw off her old, dirty robes and put on a new robe of righteousness. Not because she deserves it, mind you, but because the Father invites her—invites us—to start anew.

The prodigal son's big brother didn't like this celebration of his wayward brother's homecoming. Like the Pharisees, he held rocks of judgment in his hand ready to fire away. There will always be those who bristle at the display of grace God so freely gives. But here's the thing—big brother was also invited to the party. I'm just glad he wasn't in charge.

"Grace always runs the risk of being misused. This is a story of hope for sinners, not an excuse to be flippant about our transgressions."[6]

I believe with all my heart that this woman was forever grateful that Jesus had set her free to start anew. I believe with all my heart that's exactly what she did.

Let's go back to Laura for just a moment. After she began her new life, she followed hard after God. She was so grateful for a chance to start again that she gave her life to serving and honoring Jesus.

Sometime during her fifth year at her new church, she met a wonderful Christian man, Peter. After they were married, Laura and Peter committed their lives to serving God wherever He led. After an international missions trip, they both felt God calling them to return on a more permanent basis. Now, for more than ten years, Laura and Peter have been serving God through evangelism, discipleship, and loving people to Christ on the mission field. She has agreed with Paul when he wrote, "But one thing I do: Forgetting what is behind and straining toward what is ahead" (Philippians 3:13). Friend, that is a choice.

God doesn't just set us free *from* our past. He sets us free *to* an exciting future. And Jesus showcased the woman caught in adultery to show us how.

> *If anyone is in Christ, he is a new creation:*
> *the old has gone, the new has come!*
>
> 2 CORINTHIANS 5:17

THE WEARY WOMAN AT THE WELL

Freed from Empty Pursuits
Freed to Overflowing Purpose

The harsh midday sun beat down through a cloudless sky, and the morning breeze had long since stilled. The weary, worn woman picked up her empty water jug, a reflection of her empty life, and headed to Jacob's well to draw her daily supply.

Jacob's well was a bustling place for community life among the women in the small village. It was their one chance to leave the confines of home and mingle with friends. They caught up on the latest gossip, exchanged village news, and shared homemaking tips. Most women came to the well in groups...no surprise there. But Ramona ventured out alone.

"It would be nice if I could go to the well in the cool of the morning or the calm of the evening like all the other women," she mumbled to herself. "But it's just not worth it. I'm tired of the condescending stares, the buzzing gossip, and the snide snickers. Why, last week, Mariah yanked her five-year-old daughter's arm to keep her from getting too close to me. What? Did she think I would contaminate her if she brushed my robe? No, I prefer the searing sun to their glaring gazes."

Ramona peeked out of the door. "High noon. The coast is clear."

The Samaritan woman easily balanced the five-gallon water jug atop her veiled head and made her way to the community well. Her thoughts of rejection continued as she plodded down the dusty trail. *All I've ever wanted was to be loved. What's so wrong with that? Five times I've tried and five times I've been rejected. Married and divorced, married and divorced. Tossed away like an old sandal. Rejected by men. Shunned by former friends. I guess I'm just a pod thrown under a pig's feet that nobody really wants.*

Ramona's thoughts were interrupted as she reached her destination and noticed a lone man sitting by the well's edge. *What's a Jew like that doing in a place like this? I'll just keep my eyes down and pretend he isn't here.*

But He *was* there. And He was there for a purpose.

His unexpected words pierced the silence.

"Could I bother you for a drink?" He asked.

A Jewish man would never stoop so low as to speak to a Samaritan woman, she thought. *He's just like all other men. He won't speak to me in public where people can see, but is all too eager to engage when he wants something. I'll show him.*

With a hint of sarcasm, the woman replied. "I'm a bit confused. You are a Jew and I am a Samaritan woman, and yet you ask me for a drink? Isn't that against the rules?"

Jesus ignored her sarcasm and cut right to the chase. He was more interested in winning the woman than winning the war of words. "If you only knew who I am, you would be asking Me for a drink, and I would give you living water."

Now he had her attention. What in the world was living water? Who was this man? Without realizing it, she lowered her water jug and began lowering her emotional walls as well.

"And how are you going to get this living water?" she laughed. "You don't even have a bucket. Are you just going to reach down in the well with your hands? Our forefather, Jacob, gave us this well. Are you saying that you are greater than Jacob? That you can give us something better than he has given?"

Even though Jesus was trying to move her thinking from a physical need to spiritual truth, she was not quick to follow.

"Drink from this well," Jesus continued, "and you'll be thirsty again. But if you drink from the well that I'm speaking of, the well of living water, your thirst will be quenched forever. Not only that, you'll have a spring of water living inside you that will bubble up and spill over onto those around you."

"Give me that water!" she said. "Oh, how I'd love to never come to this well again!"

The woman didn't understand what "living water" was all about, but if it meant that she didn't have to come to the well every day and face the condemning comments and stony stares from the other women in the town, she wanted it.

"Go, get your husband and come back."

Suddenly, the warmth she had felt earlier began to seep from her soul, and the empty chill returned with a vengeance.

"I don't have a husband," she flatly replied, retreating behind a face used to hiding her emotions.

"You are right," Jesus continued. "I'm glad that you admitted it. I applaud your honesty. The truth is, you have had five husbands and the man you're living with right now is not your husband. So you are telling the truth when you say you don't have a husband."

There was not a hint of condemnation in Jesus' voice. He simply stated the facts as though He was noting the day's weather condition or the price of eggs at the market.

Suddenly the years of her pitiful life passed before her and she saw herself all alone…emotionally empty and desperately thirsty. *How did he know that about me?* She wondered. *Who is this man? Is he a prophet?*

Trying to skirt the real issue at hand, the woman tried to engage Jesus in a theological debate. She tried to divert the conversation away from her life and onto a safer subject. "Sir, I get the idea that you are a prophet. Our fathers worshipped on this mountain, but you Jews claim that the place where we must worship is in Jerusalem. Which is it?"

"Believe Me," Jesus said, "one day you will worship the Father neither on this mountain nor in Jerusalem. A time is coming and actually has now come, when the true worshippers will worship the Father in spirit and truth. That's what God really wants. It is not about where you worship, but who and how."

"Oh, well," she shrugged, "I know that Messiah is coming. When He comes, He will explain everything to us."

Jesus looked intently at the woman, and for the first time in His ministry, He told someone His true identity. "I am He."

In her heart, she knew it was true. She wanted to laugh, to cry, to worship at His feet, but before she could do any of those things, a cloud of dust and the rumble of male voices interrupted their conversation. Jesus' friends had returned from the market and stopped short, amazed that He was talking to a woman alone. But even more startling than whom He was talking to was what He had just said…"I am He."

Leaving her water pot, the woman ran back to town and told the townsfolk about the Messiah she met at Jacob's well.

A Closer Look

I have to tell you, this is one of the most exciting passages in the Bible for me. It is filled with hope for all women who feel abused, misused, and forgotten. It is for all women who have tried everything and everyone to fill the void in their hearts but still hear the echo of emptiness ring in their hollow souls.

I want you to feel the length and the depth of the words of this story. This is the longest recorded conversation between Jesus and any one single person in the entire New Testament…and it is with a woman. Let's take a seat by the edge of the well and eavesdrop a little.

> *The Pharisees heard that Jesus was gaining and baptizing*
> *more disciples than John, although in fact it was not Jesus*
> *who baptized, but his disciples. When the Lord learned of*

> *this, he left Judea and went back once more to Galilee. Now*
> *he had to go through Samaria (John 4:1-4).*

Jesus had been very busy in Judea and was on His way back to Galilee. It wasn't persecution that drove Him away, but incredible success. His increasing popularity caused Him to retreat as the Pharisees began to see Him as a threat.

The shortest route from Judea to Galilee lay on a high road straight through Samarian territory, but the Jews routinely crossed the Jordan River and took the long way around to avoid going through the towns of the despised Samaritans. In 721 BC, the Assyrians conquered Israel and deported thousands of Israelites to the land between Mount Gerizim and Ebal. There the Israelites intermarried with foreigners and became known as Samaritans.

Jews avoided Samaritans like the plague…literally. As if they were in a quarantined hospital room, the Jews kept their distance. Great prejudice and animosity existed between the two peoples. In short, they hated each other like two warring gangs.

So it wasn't because of geography that Jesus "had to go through Samaria." Oh, no. He had to go through Samaria because His Father told him to. As Jesus reminded the disciples many times, He only did what His Father told Him to do (John 5:30; 6:38; 8:26; 9:4; 10:37-38; 12:49-50).

Jesus had to go to Samaria because of divine destiny. Another translation states, "He needed to go through Samaria" (NKJV). He was there on special assignment. It was not a coincidence or a casual meeting, but a "deliberate, intentional, and calculated decision on the part of the Savior of the world to go meet with her."[1] You see, there was a woman in Samaria who had been used and abused all her life. And now God reached down from His throne and chose her for such a time as this. While she may have felt that she was damaged goods fit for no one, God chose her as His special spokesperson for an entire town. And He sent His own Son to commission her for ministry.

So Jesus had to go. Not because of geography, but because of what His Dad wrote in His celestial Day-Timer. And while the disciples went shopping for groceries, Jesus waited patiently for His assignment to come to Him.

> *So he came to a town in Samaria called Sychar, near the plot of ground Jacob had given to his son Joseph. Jacob's well was there, and Jesus, tired as he was from the journey, sat down by the well. It was about the sixth hour (John 4:5-6).*

When I was in a college film class, I remember watching an old black-and-white Western called *High Noon*. The unique feature of the movie was that it clicked along in real time. Minute by minute the plot progresses as the sheriff's wall clock ticked and the tension led up to a shoot-out at twelve o'clock sharp...high noon.

That's where we meet this leading lady. No, not on the dusty streets of Hadleyville, but on the hostile paths of Samaria...at high noon. "By Roman time it was six o'clock in the evening; by Jewish time it was twelve noon."[2] There is no gunslinging in this particular story, but there are certainly some fiery words.

John tells us, "Jacob's well was there" (John 4:6). It is still there today. If you visit the Holy Land, you can see for yourself this gathering place for the women of Jesus' day.

While most women went to the well to draw water for their daily use in the cool of the morning or late in the evening, this woman went at high noon. The scorching sun was a small price to pay in order to avoid being snubbed by the other women in the town. She preferred the heat of the sun to the cold shoulders of the women. So while the women gathered for girlfriend time at the well early in the morning, this particular woman waited until they had returned back to their safe havens in order to find safety of her own.

> *When a Samarian woman came to draw water, Jesus said to her, "Will you give me a drink?" (His disciples had gone into the town to buy food.) (John 4:7-8).*

Jesus didn't demand. He simply asked. But the fact that He even asked was radical. Jewish men didn't talk to Samaritan women. And for a Jew to drink from a Samaritan's cup was unheard of. Jews considered Samaritans unclean, and to drink from a Samaritan's cup would in turn make them unclean.

But Jesus spoke to her directly and respectfully. This was no doubt radically different from any other Jewish man she had ever come in contact with.

> *The Samaritan woman said to him, "You are a Jew and I am a Samaritan woman. How can you ask me for a drink?" (For Jews do not associate with Samaritans.) (John 4:9).*

The woman must have thought of all the times Samaritans had been treated like dirt beneath Jewish feet. This was a shocking request! Here was this Jewish man, asking for a drink from a Samaritan woman...from a Samaritan woman's cup. Scandalous.

Don't for one minute think that her nationality and gender were happenstance. They were both intentionally chosen by our very intentional God—just another example that God's plan to set the captives free was for *all* who would believe.

> *Jesus answered her, "If you knew the gift of God and who it is that asks you for a drink, you would have asked him and he would have given you living water" (John 4:10).*

What happens when someone says to you, "If you only knew?" I don't know about you, but it makes me *want to know.* Jesus spoke those same enticing words to this gal with the empty bucket. He was engaging her and inviting her to the springs of life.

The well was more than a hundred feet deep, but a little depth never stopped Jesus. God's arm is never too short. He reaches down into the deepest, darkest places of a human's soul and fills it with Himself. When we have an encounter with Him and He pours out the gift of living water, joy effervesces with the abundant life that

God intended all along. "The gift of God is eternal life in Christ Jesus our Lord" (Romans 6:23). God was holding out the package, inviting her to pluck the bow from the lid.

> "Sir," the woman said, "you have nothing to draw with and
> the well is deep. Where can you get this living water? Are
> you greater than our father Jacob, who gave us the well and
> drank from it himself, as did also his sons and his flocks and
> herds?" Jesus answered, "Everyone who drinks this water
> will be thirsty again, but whoever drinks the water I give
> him will never thirst. Indeed, the water I give him will
> become in him a spring of water welling up to eternal life"
> (John 4:11-14).

While she focused on drawing physical water, Jesus continued drawing her closer to living water. The water in Jacob's well would alleviate physical thirst temporarily. The water in Jesus' well would quench spiritual thirst eternally. Jesus' living water would fill this empty woman with overflowing joy.

Helen Keller was deaf, blind, and mute. Her tutor and caregiver, Annie Sullivan, tried and tried to teach Helen sign language by associating various words with signs she made in the girl's palm. One day, as refreshing water from an outside pump ran over Helen's hands, she realized that the cool fluid flowing over her body was the symbol that Annie made in her hand. W-a-t-e-r. "I knew then that 'w-a-t-e-r' meant the wonderful cool something that was flowing over my hand," Helen said. "That living word awakened my soul, gave it light, joy, set it free!"[3] Thus began Helen's journey of one of her most incredible discoveries—words.

When we understand the concept of living water, it has that same effect. God "awakens our soul, gives us light, joy, sets us free!" But our woman at the well wasn't quite there yet.

> The woman said to him, "Sir, give me this water so that I
> won't get thirsty and have to keep coming here to draw water"
> (John 4:15).

Wait a minute. Did she say, "Give me that water?" Isn't that what Jesus asked from her? As Jesus often does, He asked her to give Him something, only to offer something better in return. That is the very definition of redemption.

> *He told her, "Go, call your husband and come back." "I have no husband," she replied. Jesus said to her, "You are right when you say you have no husband. The fact is, you have had five husbands, and the man you now have is not your husband. What you have just said is quite true" (John 4:16-18).*

Jesus lifted the curtain on the story of her life, and the acts of the saga were exposed before her. Count them 1, 2, 3, 4, 5. Five husbands plus one extra. We don't know why she had been divorced five times. In those days, a man could divorce his wife if she went outside the home with her hair unbound or spoke to a man in public. He could even divorce her if she burnt the bread or he decided that he just didn't like her anymore. It didn't take much. But whatever the reasons, this was a woman who had been abused, misused, and tossed away by men she had trusted and loved.

This also gives us a hint that she was not a young woman. It takes time to experience that much rejection. No doubt the years of heartache and broken dreams were etched on her sun-scorched face. Like the rising bucket full of hope from the well of each new marriage, her dreams spilled out on the parched grounds of divorce—five times. Her longing for love left her empty and led her to yet another poor decision—man number six.

Jesus spoke to her of her past without a hint of condemnation or rejection in His voice. As a matter of fact, He applauded her honesty. He moved the conversation to a personal level and took one step closer to the heart of the matter…the matter of the heart. Jesus always moves the conversation to a personal level when He is about to set someone free. And He was rattling the prison keys.

> *"Sir," the woman said, "I can see that you are a prophet. Our father worshipped on this mountain, but you Jews claim that*

> *the place where we must worship is in Jerusalem" (John 4:19-*
> *20).*

What do we do when confronted with such naked truth about ourselves? Oftentimes we try to change the subject. That's exactly what this woman did. She wanted to get the spotlight off of her and onto some theological or religious debate. *"Let's don't talk about me,"* she seemed to say. *"Let's talk about religion. What about the poor people in Third World countries who have never heard the gospel? How can God allow bad things to happen to good people? What about other religions? Let's talk about that."*

Jesus always brings the subject back to me…to you. That's what is important to Him. Jesus answered her question by explaining that God is more interested in how we worship than where we worship. He is more concerned with our relationship with Him than our religious practices.

Interestingly, first she called Jesus "a Jew." Then she called him "sir." And now, confronted with the reality of her life, she calls Him "a prophet." But there was one more name she was yet to discover.

> *Jesus declared, "Believe me, woman, a time is coming when*
> *you will worship the Father neither on this mountain nor*
> *in Jerusalem. You Samaritans worship what you do not*
> *know; we worship what we do know, for salvation is from*
> *the Jews. Yet a time is coming and has now come when the*
> *true worshipers will worship the Father in spirit and truth,*
> *for they are the kind of worshipers the Father seeks. God is*
> *spirit and his worshipers must worship in spirit and in truth."*
> *The woman said, "I know that Messiah" (called Christ) "is*
> *coming. When he comes, he will explain everything to us"*
> *(John 4:21-25).*

I can see her now. She shrugs her shoulders with a dismissive "whatever" attitude. A moment later Jesus drops the bombshell.

> *Then Jesus declared, "I who speak to you am he" (John 4:26).*

In the Greek, the original language of the New Testament, the word "he" is not used in verse 26. Literally, Jesus said, "I who speak to you am."[4] This goes back to the book of Exodus, when Moses said to God,

> Suppose I go to the Israelites and say to them, "The God of your fathers has sent me to you," and they ask me, "What is his name?" Then what shall I tell them?" God said to Moses, "I AM WHO I AM. This is what you are to say to the Israelites: 'I AM has sent me to you'" (Exodus 3:13-14).

God said His name is I AM. He was. He is. And He forever will be.

When Jesus said, "I am" in John 4:26, He was equating Himself with God. Later, in John 8:58, He said, "I tell you the truth… before Abraham was born, I am!" He was expressing his eternal existence and complete oneness with God.

Never before had Jesus come right out and told someone that He was the Messiah. Never again, until the day of His trial, would He repeat those words. And yet, to this abused and misused Samaritan woman who had been rejected by man, Jesus revealed the most important truth of all creation because she was chosen by God.

> *Just then his disciples returned and were surprised to find him talking with a woman. But no one asked, "What do you want?" or "Why are you talking with her?" (John 4:27).*

Can you imagine? The disciples came back from their grocery shopping to find Jesus talking to a woman. And not just any woman, mind you, a Samaritan woman. He was breaking all the rules…again. Jesus risked His reputation to save hers. But because the disciples respected Him, they kept silent. Keeping silent never stopped Jesus from knowing what others thought. All through His ministry we see that He knew exactly what people were thinking, and this was no exception.

No doubt, these 12 men thought they were extra special. I mean, who wouldn't? They were some of Jesus' best friends—the chosen ones. But Jesus always seemed to have a way of putting them in their place. "The first shall be last." "Serve like Me." "Wash each other's feet." So here they come upon the scene of Jesus teaching a Samaritan woman and using her as a visual aid to teach them. That, my friend, was humbling. "You boys want to see how it's done? Watch this."

God's timing of the events of the day was no coincidence. If they had arrived earlier, they would have interrupted the conversation. As God would have it, they arrived just as Jesus was saying, "I who speak to you am He." She heard it. They heard it. They heard her hear it. The timing of their absence and subsequent arrival points once again to God's divine control over time and events.

By this time, the disciples had probably figured out that Jesus had His own way of doing things. But they were slow, oh so slow, to understand that part of Jesus' plan was to liberate women from the cultural, societal, and religious shackles that had them bound. Later Paul would write, "There is neither Jew nor Greek, slave nor free, male nor female, for you are all one in Christ Jesus" (Galatians 3:28).

> Then, leaving her water jar, the woman went back to the town and said to the people, "Come, see a man who told me everything I ever did. Could this be the Christ?" They came out of the town and made their way toward him (John 4:28-30).

Do you think Jesus knew where the woman was going and what she was going to do? Of course He did. He didn't try to stop her. He didn't say, "Hold up, little sister. This is just between you and Me. You can't be going out there like some kind of evangelist. Women don't do that. Nobody's going to listen to you. Just leave that job to the boys. We'll take it from here."

No. Probably with a smile on His face, Jesus watched as she left her water pot by the well like an excited child and ran back to town with the news. *Look at her go*, He must have mused. I think He may have even laughed.

Then Jesus turned to the stunned disciples. He knew what they were thinking, but rather than address their judgmental questions, He simply began using this opportunity for yet another teachable moment. He explained what was about to happen. The fields were ripe for harvest, He explained. Then He turned their attention to a newly appointed member of the workforce as she gathered in this particular crop—a woman. She collected low-hanging fruit ripe for the picking and shuttled the harvest to the Master Gardener awaiting their arrival. In effect, Jesus was saying, "Take note, boys. Pay attention. This little lady will show you how it's done." Just as He finished His lesson (John 4:31-38), the woman returned with the entire village in tow. Jesus used her actions as a teaching tool for His closest friends.

> *Many of the Samaritans from that town believed in him*
> *because of the woman's testimony, "He told me everything I*
> *ever did" (John 4:39).*

The people didn't come to Jesus because the woman entered into a theological debate with them. They came to Jesus because she told them what He had done in her life. They came because of her testimony. Revelation 12:11 says, "They [believers] overcame him [Satan], by the blood of the Lamb and the word of their testimony." Isn't it amazing that our words, the words of what Jesus has done in our lives, have enough power to even be in the same sentence with "the blood of the Lamb"?

This woman's life had been no fairy tale, but it did have a fairy-tale ending. Her Prince had come at last.

Freed from Emptiness

We all come into the world thirsty. From the time my son made his first cry in the delivery room, he began rooting around for something to drink. God planned it that way. Our bodies are 50 to 60 percent water and must be replenished continuously. When we go without water, our skin grows clammy, our eyes become scratchy, and our head starts to pound. We need water to keep our mouths moist enough to swallow, our vital organs plump enough to function, and our joints lubricated enough to flex. One week without water and we simply dry up and die.

We also come into the world spiritually thirsty. From the time we are cut loose from our mother's nourishing umbilical cord, we begin our journey to discovering the living water to satisfy the soul. Oh, we don't know it yet, but God has placed the desire in each and every one of His image bearers. Until we meet Jesus at the well, we fumble about trying to quench our God-given thirst with anything and anyone who offers temporary relief. But it is just that…temporary.

It is only in a relationship with Jesus that we discover "the ultimate purpose for which we were created, the meeting and marriage between ourselves and God…the highest and holiest and happiest hope of the human heart, the thing we were all born hungering (and thirsting) for, hunting for, longing for."[5]

The woman at the well had tried drinking from many shallow streams. But they had all left her thirsty for more—or at least for something different. Jesus offered her freely flowing, resplendently refreshing water. Water that bubbles up from the indwelling Holy Spirit and quenches every thirst, washes away every sin, and flows into every nook and cranny of our beings. He invites us to come often and drink deeply.

I live on a beautiful lake. I can look at the lake, swim in the lake, and even stand in the lake…and still die of thirst. The only way for the water to enter my system is for me to scoop it up and drink.

Likewise, we can read about Jesus, listen to sermons about Jesus, and even believe that He was a good man, but until we actually believe that Jesus is God's Son, the Messiah, who died for our sins and rose again…until we partake of Jesus and make Him Lord of our lives, we will remain thirsty.

And our woman at the well? She accepted the invitation. She believed!

In the Chronicles of Narnia, C.S. Lewis introduces a new character in *The Silver Chair*. Jill finds herself transported to Narnia as if she were caught up in a dream. The first creature she encounters is Aslan the lion, the Christ figure throughout the series. Aslan appears for a moment and then stalks slowly back into the forest. Jill is terribly afraid of meeting up with the Lion, but her increasing thirst drives her in search of water. Alas! Jill discovers a stream, but she has to pass Aslan to reach it.

"Are you not thirsty?" said the Lion.

"I'm dying of thirst," said Jill.

"Then drink," said the Lion.

"May I—could I—would you mind going away while I do?" said Jill.

The Lion answered this only by a look and a very low growl. And as Jill gazed at its motionless bulk, she realized that she might as well have asked the whole mountain to move aside for her convenience.

The delicious rippling noise of the stream was driving her nearly frantic.

"Will you promise not to—do anything to me, if I do come?" said Jill.

"I make no promise," said the Lion.

Jill was so thirsty now that, without noticing it, she had come a step nearer.

"Do you eat girls?" she said.

"I have swallowed up girls and boys, women and men, kings and emperors, cities and realms," said the Lion. It didn't say this as if it were boasting, nor as if it were sorry, nor as if it were angry. It just said it.

"I daren't come and drink," said Jill.

"Then you will die of thirst," said the Lion.

"Oh dear!" said Jill, coming another step nearer. "I suppose I must go and look for another stream then."

"There is no other stream," said the Lion.[6]

Friend, there is no other stream by which our emptiness will be truly filled. Neither people, nor places, nor possessions will satisfy the God-shaped void in our hearts. Only Jesus, the living water, will satisfy. Amazingly, He not only satisfies the thirst, but He fills the empty spaces to overflowing so that we can share the path to eternal life with others.

Freed to Overflowing Purpose

Our sister who met Jesus waiting for her by the well was set free from her emptiness and set free to overflowing purpose. Immediately she knew what she had to do...tell someone. Not that she was ordered to, but she was compelled to. Isn't it the same with you and me? We finally understand! God opens our eyes to the truth! Jesus satisfies the longing in our hearts, the longing we could never quite identify, and then we want everyone to experience that satisfaction as well. Joy bubbles up and splashes on those around us. "Come and see..." she cried. She had seen Jesus, and now the people of her village saw Jesus in her.

God had a plan for this woman. She had made some bad choices along the way, mingled with abuse and misuse by others, but that did not stop God's plan for her. Like diamonds displayed on black velvet, her dark past served as a contrasting backdrop upon which the miraculous transformation of her life would shine.

We don't know her name, but Jesus did. Not only that, He knew everything about her. He knows our names, our dreams, and our secret sins as well. Jesus knows our past, present, and future mistakes. And yet, He chooses us for specific purposes in His kingdom work. Paul tells us, "No eye has seen, no ear has heard, no mind has conceived what God has prepared for those who love him" (1 Corinthians 2:9). Nothing will stand in His way of using whomever He chooses—not even our own messy lives.

And though in those days a woman was not viewed as a credible witness, this woman was the witness that God chose to spread the good news of Jesus Christ to an entire town. She left her water jug, symbolic of her old parched life, and ran to splash the good news of the Messiah's arrival on anyone who would listen. And they believed her! It is hard to ignore a changed life. It might have been the first time God used a woman to evangelize a community, but it sure wouldn't be the last.

General William Booth, the founder of the Salvation Army said, "Some of my best men are women!"[7] In the nineteenth century, the women of the Salvation Army went through the slums of England working where the police were afraid to venture. Neighborhoods were ruled by criminals, and the streets were a breeding ground for violence and every sort of evil. But the women of the Salvation Army bravely marched onto this battleground. William's wife, Catherine, was a well-known preacher at the time. William never held her back but encouraged her to use the gifts God had given her. I can see Jesus smiling at Catherine in the dark streets of England and musing…*Look at her go.*

In the early 1800s, John and Charles Wesley led the great spiritual awakening in England and America. Their mother, Susanna, preached to more than 200 people every week in prayer meetings, which she led in her husband's parish. Later, John used women leaders for small groups called "classes," which fueled the revival. John said, "Since God uses women in the conversion of sinners, who am I that I should withstand God?"[8]

One of the most effective evangelists of our day is Anne Graham Lotz, the daughter of Billy Graham. Both Mr. Graham and his son Franklin agree that Anne is the best preacher in the family.[9] But when Anne spoke at a 1988 pastors' conference, some men turned their chairs around and placed their backs to the stage. Their act was in protest to a woman evangelist. Anne doesn't try to convince people about her call to teach or evangelize. "When people have a problem with women in ministry," she said in an interview, "they need to take it up with Jesus. He's the one who put us here."

How thankful I am to Dr. Henrietta Mears of Hollywood's First Presbyterian Church in Los Angeles, who led a Bible study which a young man named Bill Bright attended. Under her teaching, Bright gave his life to Christ. He later went on to establish Campus Crusade for Christ, an organization that has helped lead an estimated 54.5 million people to Jesus. Since 1951, the ministry of Campus Crusade has brought more than 4.5 billion "exposures" to the gospel worldwide.[10]

Billy Graham, who was mentored by Henrietta Mears, had this to say:

> I have known Dr. Henrietta Mears for approximately fifteen years. She has had a remarkable influence, both directly and indirectly on my life. In fact, I doubt if any other woman outside of my wife and my mother has had such a marked influence. Her gracious spirit, her devotional life, her steadfastness for the simple gospel, and her knowledge of the Bible have been a continual inspiration and amazement to me. She is certainly one of the greatest Christians I have ever known.[11]

Henrietta Mears never married or bore children of her own, but she had great significance in the kingdom of God. She threw herself into God's purposes for her generation and what a crop she produced! What a woman!

I'll never forget when I spoke at a retreat in Massachusetts. About 300 women had gathered in a hotel for a weekend of praise, prayer, and preaching. We opened our Bibles together, joined hands in prayer, and blended voices in praise. Among the 300 women, in a far corner of the room, sat one man who ran the sound system. From the very beginning session on Friday night, God pricked my heart to pray for George.

Sunday morning, we all stood and praised God for His amazing transforming work among the women over the past 48 hours. We especially thanked God for our new brother-in-Christ—George. On Sunday morning, George accepted Jesus as his Savior. God used the teaching, the testimonies, and the tender hearts of women who prayed to lead this man to the well—to Jesus. He believed and joined the family of God.

Imagine that. God used women, an army of evangelists, to enlist God's latest recruit. "The women who proclaim the good tidings are a great host" (Psalm 68:11 NASB).

Our friend at the well had been a social outcast, but Jesus cast His net and drew her in. He replaced her feelings of rejection with a sense of respect, and He used her as the catalyst for the salvation of many.

The disciples went into town because they were hungry. The woman went into town to get hungry people. She was no longer a second-class citizen relegated to the back row of the balcony; now she had a front row seat to the greatest show on earth. And at just the right moment, Jesus pulled her from the crowd and placed her center stage to play a leading role.

Why did John include this story in his Gospel? As with all of the accounts he could have included: "These things are written that you may come to believe that Jesus is the Messiah, the Son of God, and that by believing you may have life in his name" (John 20:31). I think God made sure this story was included just for me...and you. Radical! Amazing! Liberating!

One thing John forgot to tell us—the woman's name. I'm so glad. I've called her Ramona in my retelling of the events, but that is just to help us see her as a real person. Her name is my name. Her name is your name. Jesus offers living water to everyone who will meet Him at the well to receive, and then He commissions us to share that water with others. Jesus freed her from a life of emptiness and freed her to a life of overflowing purpose.

Whoever is thirsty, let him come; and whoever
wishes, let him take the free gift of the water of life.

REVELATION 22:17

7

THE WINSOME WORSHIPPER

Freed from a Painful Past
Freed to Pour Out Praise

ave you heard," the vender at the marketplace whispered. "Jesus is in town and He is having dinner at Simon's house!" Upon hearing the news, Bethany's heart quickened as she remembered the first time she saw Jesus.

She had been among the crowd at the temple court when the religious leaders interrupted Jesus' teaching and dragged a half-dressed woman caught in the act of adultery before them. The Pharisees displayed the woman like a prize catch. Jesus and the Pharisees engaged in conversation about the situation and what was to be done to the adulteress. Then Jesus squatted down and wrote something in the dirt.

Then He said, "Let he who is without sin throw the first stone."

One by one the men dropped their stones and walked away. Bethany moved closer to the front so she wouldn't miss what Jesus would say to the accused.

"Has no one condemned you?" Jesus asked.

"No one, sir," she replied.

"Then neither do I condemn you. Go and sin no more."

Bethany felt as if Jesus had spoken directly to her, even though she hid behind her veil among the crowd. Then Jesus turned as if He knew exactly where she was hiding and met her gaze. Without a word, it was as if He said, "This grace is extended to you too, my friend."

Bethany recalled other teachings of Jesus:

> Do not judge, or you too will be judged…and with the measure you use, it will be measured to you. Why do you look at the speck of sawdust in your brother's eye and pay no attention to the plank in your own eye?…It is not the healthy who need a doctor, but the sick…For I have not come to call the righteous, but sinners…Your sins are forgiven…Get up, take your mat, and go home.[1]

Like the man who had been paralyzed, she too had been paralyzed and crippled, but in a different way. She felt trapped in a cycle of sin from which she could not break free. But each time she heard Jesus speak, the jingle of the keys to freedom drew her near.

The buzz around town was "Who is this who forgives sins?"

She knew. In her heart she knew that this was the promised Messiah, the one of whom Isaiah spoke. Hadn't Jesus even quoted Isaiah?

> The Spirit of the Lord is on me, because he has anointed me to preach good news to the poor. He has sent me to proclaim freedom for the prisoners and recovery of sight to the blind, to release the oppressed, and to proclaim the year of the LORD's favor.[2]

Isaiah had described her perfectly: poor, brokenhearted, captive, prisoner, mournful, grieving, and despairing. *If Jesus could forgive the woman caught in adultery and the lame man on his pallet, perhaps He could forgive me as well*, Bethany hoped.

Oh, how she longed to be free of her past. Free of the shame and condemnation that followed her sinful and perverted lifestyle. Free from the shunning silence and loathing looks of the village women. Free from the abuse and misuse of her body among the men willing to pay for a few moments of pleasure. Free from the sickness of her soul.

Now, hearing that He was in town, she was compelled to run to Him and worship the One who could set her free.

"I must go to Him," she whispered, "but I can't go to Him empty handed. What gift could I take this holy man?"

Her gaze left the dirt floor and settled on the alabaster jar resting on the roughly hewn mantle. Her ability to show true love had been sealed shut like the ointment in this fragile container. Cold. Hard. Impermeable.

She held the fine Egyptian marble in her hand. The delicately carved cream-colored vial contained pure nard, an undiluted costly perfume. The feathery veins of the stone reminded her of the twisted and convoluted roads of her life, and the cold hard stone mirrored her hardened heart. But then she remembered how one look from Jesus had begun to warm and penetrate the glacial surface of her soul. Each remembrance chipped away at the protective stone that defined her. "'Then neither do I condemn you.' That's what He said," she whispered.

Though small enough to fit in the palm of her hand, the vial's fragrant content was strong enough to permeate a room. It was her only valuable possession. *What can I give Him?* she asked herself. *I'll give Him all I have.*

The woman pushed through the crowds on the dusty streets of Capernaum. "Have you seen Him? Have you seen Him?" she asked. "I heard that Jesus was in town. Do you know where He is?"

"Yes," someone sneered. "But what would He want with the likes of you?"

"Where is He?" she begged. "Please tell me. Where is He?"

"He is having dinner at Simon the Pharisee's house, but you'll not be welcomed there."

Ignoring the warning, she picked up the corners of her robe, clutched the small jar to her breast, and ran to the familiar house of the Pharisee. Bethany burst through the wooden doors and panned the room for Jesus.

"You can't go in there," someone called out. "Women aren't allowed inside. You'll have to stand out here like the rest of us to pick up any scraps that are left behind."

They didn't understand that she was not coming to get food. She was coming to give praise.

Then she saw Him. There He was. Reclining at the crowded table on His left side with His feet tucked behind him.

As if they were the only two people in the room, Bethany walked slowly and intentionally toward Him. Transfixed on her Savior, she purposefully advanced. The men began to turn from their conversations and visually follow her across the room. Some of them knew her by reputation; some because they had been paying customers.

Slowly, ignoring the condescending stares of the all-male dinner guests, she gingerly knelt beside Jesus and cupped His feet in her hands. His precious feet. Tears pooled in her eyes and then began trickling like raindrops. Soon salty streams cut through the caked-on mud as years of pent up anguish released and gushed forth in an endless flow. Scandalously, in an act reserved only for a husband, Bethany pulled the pins from her raven hair and let it cascade over her shoulders. Then she took the tresses and gently wiped Jesus' feet. All the while, tears of gratitude and worship streamed down her weathered cheeks as she covered her Savior's feet with kisses.

A hush filled the room and all eyes were fixed on this woman kneeling at Jesus' feet. All male eyes. Gawking eyes.

Still weeping, the woman pulled the alabaster jar from the folds of her robe. Love bubbled up within her and demanded release as she broke the neck of the alabaster jar. The perfume she had once used to lure men for a night of sinful passion she now emptied on the One who lured her with a life of glorious grace.

As the jar was broken, she became whole. The scent of the treasured nard escaped the vial and encircled the room. She poured its contents onto her beloved Master's feet. All of it. The fragrance of grace circled the room and clung to the unsuspecting crowd.

After a brief conversation with Simon, Jesus placed His hand on Bethany's head and gently spoke. "Your sins are forgiven. Your faith has saved you; go in peace."

A Closer Look

Who was this woman? Why did she cross the gender boundary lines and brave the condemning crowd to see Jesus? What was the significance of the perfume? What can we learn from her courageous act? Let's take a closer look at how Luke described the scene.

> *One of the Pharisees invited Jesus to have dinner with him,*
> *so he went to the Pharisee's house and reclined at the table*
> *(Luke 7:36).*

Simon was a Pharisee—a religious leader. The name "Pharisee" actu-ally means "separated or pious ones." As teachers of the law, they separated themselves from the unrighteous or unclean. They set up strict boundaries between holy and ordinary people. They did not allow unrighteous people to touch them. Of course, they were the ones who defined who was and was not righteous, which was not right at all.

But as we know, our sweet Jesus disregarded man-made boundaries and stepped right into human hearts. He was no ordinary man, but One who came to save ordinary people like you and me. From the shepherds on the hillside who were the first to hear the good news of His birth to the woman at the tomb who was the first to receive the good news of His resurrection—ordinary people all.

But on this occasion, Jesus was having dinner with the very group that would soon have Him put to death.

> *When a woman who had lived a sinful life in that town*
> *learned that Jesus was eating at the Pharisee's house, she*
> *brought an alabaster jar of perfume, and as she stood behind*
> *him at his feet weeping, she began to wet his feet with her*
> *tears (Luke 7:37-38).*

Here we have yet another woman with no name. I have called her Bethany just to help us grasp the fact that this was a real flesh-and-blood woman, not just a character in a story. I am particularly drawn to these nameless gals because we can fill in the blank with our own names. She was referred to as "the sinful woman," "the woman who anointed Jesus," or "the woman with the alabaster jar."

The Amplified Bible calls her "an especially wicked sinner," "a noto-rious sinner," and "a social outcast, devoted to sin." The New Living Translation describes her as " a certain immoral woman."

The truth is, Luke doesn't say she was a prostitute. Scholars have assumed she was. What she did for a living is not really the point. She could have been a thief or even a gossip. This is a story about a woman who was a sinner and Jesus who forgave her. She is a woman whose gratitude overflowed with a selfless act of love. That's what is at stake here. Not the particular sin.

The "sin" that defined her could have been any number of things. If we fixate on the speculation of her being a prostitute, we miss the point. Unless you are a prostitute, you may have trouble seeing Jesus through her eyes. So let's take that label off of her for now. Let's just see her as Luke intended—a sinful woman.

Now, can you see yourself walking into a room full of gawk-ing men? Can you taste salty tears? Can you feel the gratitude of a woman set free bubbling up within you? Can you humbly crouch at Jesus' feet with her? I hope so. There's no better place to be.

We don't know exactly where this particular woman first met Jesus. It could have been at the temple when the Pharisees brought the woman caught in adultery. It could have been at any number of His teaching sites or His miraculous healings. We don't know where or when, but we do know that at some point she had encountered His forgiving grace.

And let's not forget the specifics of her intrusion. Women were not allowed to eat with the men. They were not even allowed to serve at gatherings such as this one. It was a boys-only event all the way around. And yet this courageous woman stepped right across the forbidden threshold. Not only did Jesus welcome her in, but He invited her to join Him at the head table.

> *Then she wiped them with her hair, kissed them and poured perfume on them (Luke 7:38).*

As I mentioned before, in this culture women kept their hair bound up. To let one's hair down in public was scandalous and grounds for divorce. Loose, flowing hair was considered seductive and reserved only for a husband in the privacy of his own home. But this woman didn't care about society's rules or what others thought of her. All she cared about was worshipping Jesus. Using her dark tresses as a hand towel, she dried His feet and patted away her tears.

But she wasn't quite finished. She had one more act of worship to perform. Extravagantly, she cracked the neck of the alabaster jar and poured the entire contents on Jesus' feet.

> *When the Pharisee who had invited him saw this, he said to himself, "If this man were a prophet, he would know who is touching him and what kind of woman she is—that she is a sinner" (Luke 7:39).*

Simon was not too happy with the intrusion of this well-known sinful woman. He certainly was disappointed in Jesus' reaction to her.

Jesus knew what Simon was thinking. All through the New Testament we read of Jesus knowing people's thoughts. After Jesus forgave the paralytic's sins, Jesus knew what the teachers of the Law were thinking (Mark 2:8). When Jesus healed the man with the withered hand on the Sabbath in front of the Pharisees, He "knew what they were thinking" (Luke 6:8). And even though a hush fell on this room of men watching this weeping woman worship at Jesus' feet, the Master heard every thought not uttered.

Simon doubted Jesus' divinity because He allowed this sinner to touch Him, as if He didn't know what sort of woman she was. Jesus proved His divinity by responding to Simon's unspoken thoughts. Not only did Jesus know what kind of women she was, He also knew what kind of man the Pharisee was. Simon thought Jesus should have corrected the woman, but instead Jesus corrected him.

> *Jesus answered him, "Simon, I have something to tell you."*
> *"Tell me, teacher," he said. "Two men owed money to a certain moneylender. One owed him five hundred denarii,*

*and the other fifty. Neither of them had the money to pay
him back, so he canceled the debts of both. Now which of
them will love him more?" Simon replied, "I suppose the
one who had the bigger debt canceled." "You have judged
correctly," Jesus said. Then he turned toward the woman and
said to Simon, "Do you see this woman?" (Luke 7:40-44).*

Let's stop and think about five little words that changed this
woman's life. "Do you see this woman?" Jesus asked.

In her book *Bad Girls of the Bible*, Liz Curtis Higgs points out
that "Simon had seen her, but only for *what* she was, not *who* she
was. He had looked at her form but not her face. He had eyed
her actions but not looked her in the eye and connected with her,
human to human."[3]

Simon saw a sinner. Jesus saw a repentant child of God. Jesus saw
her...the real her. He looked past the sullied reputation and saw the
sincere heart. Our God is El Roi, the God Who Sees, and He saw
this precious woman kneeling at her Savior's feet.

She knew rejection. She knew what it was like to be invited to
a party only to be used by the men who were present there. Jesus
understood that as well. He was surrounded by people who only saw
what they could squeeze out of Him rather than who He really was.
Physical healing. Free bread. Water to wine. Mental health. Used?
Jesus understood *used*.

All her life men had used her and women had treated her with disgust. But Jesus welcomed her worship, accepted her adoration, and
honored her humility. Not once did He recoil or refuse her touch.

*I came into your house. You did not give me any water for my
feet, but she wet my feet with her tears and wiped them with
her hair. You did not give me a kiss, but this woman, from
the time I entered, has not stopped kissing my feet. You did
not put oil on my head, but she has poured perfume on my
feet. Therefore, I tell you, her many sins have been forgiven—
for she loved much. But he who has been forgiven little loves
little (Luke 7:44-47).*

Simon invited Jesus to dinner but then paid little attention to Him. The religious leaders made a good show, but they forgot to acknowledge the honored guest. Happens all the time in churches all around the world. People get caught up in the service and programs and forget to acknowledge and worship the honored guest... if He's invited at all.

But then someone came who hadn't forgotten Him. A woman. A sinful woman. A social outcast. And she anointed Him with perfume.

Perfume was very expensive and hard to come by in those days. Most originated from plant sources, none of which naturally grew in the Holy Land. They had to be imported from Arabia, Iran, India, and elsewhere.[4]

Hosts often put a few drops of oil on their guests' heads as a show of hospitality. I imagine it certainly helped the smell of a room full of people that lacked the convenience of indoor plumbing and daily showers.

But this woman did not simply dole out a few drops of costly nard on Jesus' head. She poured out the entire vial. All of it.

In a few months' time, Jesus would pay an exorbitant price for our eternal freedom. But at this moment, the woman gave all she had in gratitude for hers.

It was a scene of contrasts.

Simon did not welcome Jesus with the customary kiss. The woman had not stopped kissing Jesus' feet since the time she entered.

Simon did not offer water to wash Jesus' feet. The woman washed His feet with her tears.

Simon did not put the traditional oil on his guest's head. The woman poured an entire vial on His feet.

Simon looked on with condemnation. The woman overflowed with love.

Simon did not give Jesus anything. The woman gave all she had.

This woman asked for nothing but received everything. She found healing in the home of a hypocrite. As with the woman at the well, Jesus shown the spotlight on a woman to teach what true worship looks like.

> *Then Jesus said to her, "Your sins are forgiven...Your faith has saved you; go in peace" (Luke 8:48,50)*

As the woman's tears cleansed Jesus' feet, His words cleansed her soul. It was not what she did that saved her, but rather what she believed. She didn't say a word, but her actions spoke volumes. Jesus knew what was in her heart just as surely as He knew what was in Simon's.

Paul wrote, "It is by grace you have been saved, through faith—and this not from yourselves, it is the gift of God—not by works, so that no one can boast" (Ephesians 2:8-9). Remember, grace is a gift we don't deserve or earn. We receive it by faith. She didn't earn salvation by her actions but received the gift by faith.

Finally, Jesus said, "Go in peace." Peace always follows forgiveness. Like the woman caught in adultery, she was free to start anew.

When we come to Jesus, He always turns our lives around and commands us to go. The Amplified Bible phrases it this way: "Go (enter) into peace (untroubled, undisturbed well-being)." She was freed from a shameful past. She was freed to pour out praise.

Freed from a Painful Past

Several years ago I was teaching at a women's conference. During the times when I was not speaking, I sat in the crowd with the attendees. In one particular session, a gal named Lisa sat in front of me. During the worship times, Lisa raised her hands and praised God as if the two of them were the only ones in the room. "Thank You, Jesus!" she cried at various intervals.

Some were bothered by this outward demonstration of praise. Others wore a knowing smile.

Later I chatted with Lisa and she told me her story. "I took my first drink when I was 13, lost my virginity at 14, and smoked marijuana for the first time that same year," she began. "For the next 28 years I chased after anything and everything to numb the pain in my life and transport me to a different world...if only temporarily. After high school, I worked as a bartender and was beaten by my boyfriend on a regular basis. Eventually, I started using cocaine. Cocaine is very expensive, and I needed a way to support my habit, so I became a prostitute. With every trick, a part of me died. Eventually, I became numb to it all. Amazingly, I was arrested for writing bad checks, not prostitution. My attorney got me out of jail and into a recovery program. While I was there, I met Jesus Christ. It was Jesus who set me free and that's the only reason I am alive today."[5]

When I met Lisa, she was a married mother of two and serving as a women's ministry director in a growing and vibrant church. Now tell me, does she have something to praise God about? Absolutely!

Maybe you have not been redeemed from a life of prostitution or drug addiction, but you and I both have been redeemed from a life of sin and condemnation just the same. We all make mistakes... just different ones.

The church is full of men and women who look back on the past with some regret. One poor choice: a walk into an abortion clinic, a one-night stand at a college party, a click on the computer keyboard. These are self-inflicted wounds that need the healing touch of Jehovah Rapha—the One Who Heals.

The Bible tells us that before we knew Christ, we were:

- Dead in our transgressions and sin (Ephesians 2:1)
- Far away from God (Ephesians 2:13)
- Separated from Christ and without hope (Ephesians 2:12)
- Enemies of God (Colossians 1:21)
- Living in darkness (1 Thessalonians 5:4)
- Darkness personified (Ephesians 5:8)
- Slaves of sin (Romans 6:17)
- Condemned (Romans 8:3)
- Unable to please God (Romans 8:8)

And now, because of the finished work of Jesus Christ on the cross and our decision to follow Him, we are:

- Alive with Christ (Colossians 2:13)
- More than conquerors (Romans 8:37)
- Reconciled to God (2 Corinthians 5:18-19)
- Joined with Christ (1 Corinthians 6:17 NKJV)
- Friends of God (John 15:15)
- Living in the light of Christ (1 Peter 2:9)
- Light personified (Matthew 5:14)
- Slaves of righteousness (Romans 6:18)
- Accepted (Romans 15:7)
- Justified (Romans 5:9)
- Redeemed (Galatians 3:13)
- Sanctified (1 Corinthians 6:11)
- Washed (1 Corinthians 6:11)
- Forgiven (1 John1:9)
- Sealed (Ephesians 1:13)
- Free (Romans 8:2)
- Complete (Colossians 2:10 NKJV)

Now tell me, do we have something to praise God about? I can hardly contain myself!

Freed to Pour Out Praise

I was speaking at a conference in New York, and my friend Gwen Smith was leading worship. Gwen and I both love worshipping the Lord openly and freely, and there's nothing better than a room full of women joining in. However, at this particular event, it became apparent that the women were a bit reserved. We both felt a slight chill in the air as words came from their mouths, but not their hearts. The best way I know to describe it is lukewarm. And we all know how God feels about lukewarm: "Because you are lukewarm—neither hot nor cold—I am about to spit you out of my mouth" (Revelation 3:16).

But over to my right, positioned on the front row, secured in her wheelchair, sat a middle-aged, African-American woman with cerebral palsy. And even though her body was twisted and contorted, even though a friend was there to dab the drool that inadvertently dripped from her lips, even though she could not pronounce the words clearly...this woman praised God with all her might. She didn't care what anyone thought. When it came to worship, it was between her and her Jesus.

She loved Jesus! She absolutely loved Him! And it showed.

My eyes filled with tears as I glanced around the room to see all of us, so richly blessed, who worshipped like halfhearted believers more concerned with what others thought than what God deserves. Just as the woman with the alabaster box poured out her praise and adoration to the One who set her free, this body-bound, spiritually free child of God poured out her praise and adoration on the One she loved most.

"How can I not praise Him," she later told me through halted and strained speech. "He has done so much for me. I just wish I could do more for Him. I want to do so much more."

For the rest of the weekend I praised God with all I had in me. And you know what? I watched walls of self-consciousness crumble all around. Women who had been closet hand-raisers lifted their hands high, sang to God rather than to the screen, and wept tears of gratitude to the One who says, "Your sins are forgiven. Your faith has saved you. Go in peace."

One little physically challenged child of God opened her alabaster jar of praise and the fragrance permeated everyone in the room. Her poured-out praise made us want to fall at Jesus' feet.

She didn't care what anyone thought of her. Her only concern was letting Jesus know what she thought of Him. I want to be like that, don't you? So what if someone thinks I'm a fanatic for raising my hands during worship. So what if they think my voice is off-key when singing to the Lord at the top of my lungs. And clapping? Didn't the psalmist say, "Clap your hands, all you peoples! Shout to God with the voice of triumph!" (Psalm 47:1)? Where did all the clapping go? Who silenced the shouts of praise? Who drew the line between reverberating praise and reverence and said they could not coexist? And dancing before the Lord? Some even look on with disgust at a gentle sway.

Regardless of what others may think, we are freed to worship at Jesus' feet! I call that winsome worship—engaging, delightful, enjoyable, lovely, exquisite, graceful worship. Listen to these verses from a man who knew how to praise God with all he had:

> I will praise you, O LORD, with all my heart; I will tell of all your wonders. I will be glad and rejoice in you; I will sing praise to your name, O Most High (Psalm 9:1-2).

> The LORD lives! Praise be to my Rock! (Psalm 18:46).

> Praise the LORD with the harp; make music to him on the ten-stringed lyre. Sing to him a new song; play skillfully, and shout for joy (Psalm 33:2-3).

> I will praise you, O Lord, among the nations; I will sing of you among the peoples. For great is your love, reaching to the heavens; your faithfulness reaches to the skies (Psalm 57:9-10).

> I will praise you as long as I live, and in your name I will lift up my hands (Psalm 63:4).

> I cried out to him with my mouth; his praise was on my tongue…Praise be to God, who has not rejected my prayer or withheld his love from me! (Psalm 66:17,20).

> Praise be to the Lord, to God our Savior, who daily bears our burdens (Psalm 68:19).

> From birth I have relied on you; you brought me forth from my mother's womb. I will ever praise you. I have

become like a portent to many, but you are my strong refuge. My mouth is filled with your praise, declaring your splendor all day long (Psalm 71:6-8).

My lips will shout for joy when I sing praise to you—I, whom you have redeemed (Psalm 71:23).

I will praise you, O Lord my God, with all my heart; I will glorify your name forever (Psalm 86:12).

Praise the LORD (Psalm 103:1,2,20,21,22; 104:1,35; 106:48; 108:3).

Lift up your hands in the sanctuary and praise the LORD (Psalm 134:2).

And here's one of my favorite noisy Psalms:

Praise the LORD. Praise God in his sanctuary; praise him in his mighty heavens. Praise him for his acts of power; praise him for his surpassing greatness. Praise him with the sounding of the trumpet, praise him with the harp and lyre, praise him with tambourine and dancing, praise him with the strings and flute, praise him with the clash of cymbals, praise him with resounding cymbals. Let everything that has breath praise the LORD. Praise the LORD (Psalm 150:1-6).

We can learn so much from the "sinful woman" who washed Jesus' feet with her tears, dried them with her hair, and anointed them with perfume. Her name is our name. Jesus forgave our sins, welcomes our worship, and promises us peace. We have been set free from our painful past and set free to pour praise for Him.

God called our sister out of the shadows of society to show all of us what the poured-out praise of a sinner set free looks like. Sure, it caused a buzz among the folks who were watching, and sister, we're still talking about her today. That's what happens when God calls a woman center stage and she obeys.

If the Son sets you free, you will be free indeed.

JOHN 8:36

8

The Daring Disciple
(Mary of Bethany)

Freed from Others' Expectations
Freed to Accept God's Invitation

Mary and Martha lived in a home with their brother, Lazarus, in the small Judean village of Bethany. Bethany was two miles east of the temple in Jerusalem, on the east slope of the Mount of Olives—the final station on the road from Jericho to Jerusalem. "Bethany" meant "house of dates and figs," the perfect place to stop for refreshment. Mary and Martha's home served as a safe haven and quiet retreat for Jesus as he traveled from place to place.

Mary takes center stage three times in Jesus' earthly ministry. We'll take a look at two of these encounters to discover how Jesus set women free *from* past prejudices that kept them from being students of God's Word, and freed *to* become disciples of Christ and learn the deep truths of Scripture. The third will be covered in the next chapter as we look at Mary's older sister, Martha.

Let's join Jesus at His first encounter with Mary of Bethany, in her home where a special feast was being prepared. The welcome mat is freshly swept, the aroma from the kitchen is wafting from the windows, and the chatter from the group of men lets us know that friends are within. But Jesus is serving up something extra special for the girls.

Daring Disciple
Mary and Martha were busy in the kitchen making dinner for

their honored guest and His friends. "Mary, check on the roasting lamb," Martha called among the clattering of the pots and pans. "And where's the wine? The bread must be kneaded in 15 minutes. There's just so much to do!"

"I'll take a bowl of fresh dates in to the guests," Mary said. "That will give them something to nibble on while we finish the preparations."

As Mary entered the room, she heard Jesus talking about the kingdom of God, the plan of redemption, the fulfillment of prophecy, the forgiveness of sins, and eternal life.

"Do not judge, and you will not be judged," Jesus taught. "Do not condemn, and you will not be condemned. Forgive and you will be forgiven. Give, and it will be given to you.

"The kingdom of God is like a mustard seed, which a man took and planted in his garden. It grew and became a tree, and the birds of the air perched in its branches."

Jesus noticed Mary standing in the doorway and motioned for her to enter. Looking directly at her, He continued, "The kingdom of God is like yeast that a woman took and mixed into a large amount of flour until it worked all through the dough."

Jesus continued teaching about who He was and what He came to do. Mesmerized by the Rabbi's words, Mary sank to the floor and sat right at the Master's feet with the others. The men shifted uncomfortably in their places, but Jesus lowered His eyes and began speaking directly to Mary—His newest student.

The disciples waited for Jesus to send Mary back into the kitchen where she belonged, but He didn't. They were confused when Jesus welcomed her in the classroom, but they tried their best not to become distracted by her presence. After all, women were not allowed to sit and learn from a rabbi's teaching. They weren't even allowed to join men in such a gathering at all.

Twenty minutes passed before Martha huffed, "Where is that girl!"

She angrily stomped into the gathering room with mixing bowl in hand. All eyes turned toward the frustrated sister as she interrupted Jesus and pointed her wooden spoon in Mary's direction.

"Lord," she began sternly, "can't you see that Mary has left me all alone in the kitchen? What does she think she's doing? Don't You care that I have to do all this work by myself while my irresponsible sister is out here lollygagging about with the men? Why, she's not even supposed to be out here at all. It isn't proper for a woman to join a room full of men, much less sit at a rabbi's feet while he's teaching. Put her in her place! Tell her to get back in the kitchen this instant!"

The men turned their head from Jesus to the red-faced Martha and back to Jesus again.

"Martha, Martha," Jesus replied, "don't get so worked up. Mary is right where she needs to be. You are so worried, bothered, and distracted with the details of living that you miss the joys of life. You don't need to work so hard to create a feast for us. That's not even important. What *is* important is that I am here and have something to share with you. Mary has figured that out. She has chosen what is important, and I am not going to send her away. She has joined the classroom to learn—to become a disciple of God's Word—and I am not going to take that away from her."

Martha put her flour-covered hand on her hip, spun around on her heels, and marched back into the kitchen. "Well, I never," she mumbled as she stomped away.

A Closer Look

Several facets of this story just tickle me. Call me mischievous, but I get the giggles when I think about Martha trying to put Mary in her place, and then Jesus putting Martha in hers. Let's take a closer look.

> As Jesus and his disciples were on their way, he came to a village where a woman named Martha opened her home to him (Luke 10:38).

Most likely, because Martha's name was mentioned first, she was the older of the two sisters and hostess for the evening. Luke didn't mention it here, but Martha and Mary had a brother named Lazarus, who we will later discover was one of Jesus' closest friends.

> *She had a sister called Mary, who sat at the Lord's feet*
> *listening to what he said (Luke 10:39).*

So that we can fully understand the incredible freedom that Jesus bestowed on Mary of Bethany in His invitation to sit at His feet as a pupil, let's review how women were viewed in that particular culture.

Remember, during this time in history, women were not allowed to be taught by the rabbis. In the ancient synagogues, women were permitted to listen, but only men were expected to learn. It was a common belief that teaching women was a waste of time and they were incapable of learning.[1]

Josephus, a noted Jewish historian, wrote that a woman "is in every respect less worth than a man!"[2] Women were put in a category with children and slaves. They were viewed as incapable of comprehending religious matters. Rabbi Eliezer ben Azariah taught, "It is better that the words of the law should be burned than that they should be given to a woman."[3] This is the general attitude toward women when we meet Mary.

In our culture, to sit at someone's feet conjures up a picture of children gathered around the feet of a storyteller or teacher. However, to the first-century Jew, to sit at someone's feet was to take the position of a student being taught. It was a sign of respect and readiness to learn, and it was the position of higher learning. Often teachers sat on a raised platform and students clustered below on the floor. Paul referred to this position when he announced to a hostile crowd that he was taught "at the feet of Gamaliel" (Acts 22:3 KJV).

When Luke tells us that Mary was sitting at Jesus' feet, the first-century reader would have understood that she was taking the position of a student in a classroom right along with the men. This was unheard of. It simply was not done.

When I was a child, one of my favorite activities was the Hidden Pictures pages in the *Highlights* magazines often found in doctors' waiting rooms. The task was to find objects out of place. A car in a tree. A hairbrush in a bowl of soup. A dog sitting at a desk. This picture of Mary sitting at Jesus' feet would have been like the Hidden Pictures page in a *Highlights* magazine. To the men at the dinner party, something was strangely out of place. Something did not belong.

But Jesus was the great Liberator, and He came to liberate women from the religious gender prejudice that kept them from theological studies. Jesus invited women to learn about the One who loved them most—to become theologians in their own right. Mary was an *ezer* who needed to be readied for battle. Jesus was teaching and equipping her for the greatest battle ever fought, and she was an eager soldier volunteering for active duty.

> But Martha was distracted by all the preparations that had to be made. She came to him and asked, "Lord, don't you care that my sister has left me to do the work by myself?" (Luke 10:40).

Amazingly, it was not the men who complained. It was Mary's own sister—another woman. Martha was the one who caused the ruckus. "Tell her to get back in here and help me!" she complained.

Martha was mad, and I can understand that. One Thanksgiving I had 38 people for the dinner. I would have been fit to be tied if I had been left to serve all those people by myself. I understand her frustration. But I love Martha so much, we're going to let her have a chapter all to herself. Let's stick with Mary at the moment.

> "Martha, Martha," the Lord answered, "you are worried and upset about many things, but only one thing is needed. Mary has chosen what is better and it will not be taken away from her" (Luke 10:41-42).

Boy, was Martha surprised when Jesus applauded Mary's choice to join Him in the classroom. An all-male classroom, I might add. Women had been sequestered in the kitchen far too long. Jesus invited Mary to put down the pots and pans and to pick up paper and pen.

He assured His newest pupil and Martha—and you and me, for that matter—that Mary was not out of order. She was exactly where she needed to be.

By reprimanding Martha, Jesus sends a clear message to us all. Life is crammed with activities we deem necessary, but knowing Jesus supersedes everything else that shouts for our attention. "More than simply granting women permission to learn as his disciples, Jesus calls Mary, Martha, and the rest of us to make knowing God our highest priority."[4]

Purposeful Prophet

Mary shares scene 2 with her sister, Martha, playing a greater role, so we will skip ahead for now, and join Mary in scene 3 of her recorded times with Jesus.

Once again, we find Jesus at a dinner party. As usual, the men are gathered around the table and the women are absent from the scene...that is until Mary enters the room...again. Only this time she is not there to learn. She is there to teach.

Martha and Mary were hosting a dinner party for Jesus and His closest friends. The party was not at their home, but Simon had convinced Martha to be in charge of all the fixings. After all, there was no one better at hosting a party than Martha.

But this was a special celebration—no ordinary dinner party. Only months before, Martha and Mary had been mourning their brother, Lazarus' death. And now? And now, because of Jesus, Lazarus sat alive and well amongst his friends. He was most likely laughing and telling jokes as though he'd never seen the inside of a darkened tomb for four days. What a celebration!

"Mary, don't forget to stir the lamb stew," Martha called from across the room. "Our guests will be here any minute."

How kind of Simon the Leper to open his home to us, Mary mused. *Oh, we must do something about his name. After all, he doesn't have leprosy any longer. Jesus healed him months ago. Just look at his skin—smooth as a newborn babe's. If he were still Simon the Leper, none of us would be here.*

As Mary continued to stir the stew, her mind began to stir with memories of Jesus' past three years: the helpless healed, the demon-possessed delivered, the rotting raised, the rejected restored, and the sinner saved. But Mary's soaring soul began a gradual descent as she remembered Jesus' words about His eminent death: "The Son of Man will be betrayed to the chief priests and the teachers of the law. They will condemn Him to death and will turn Him over to the Gentiles to be mocked and flogged and crucified. On the third day He will be raised to life!"[5]

I know our time with Him is short, she thought. *I can't bear the thought of losing Him, and yet, I know that is why He came. That is what He has taught us all along. My heart is so heavy. What can I do to honor Him?*

Mary's mind traveled to another incident in Jesus' life. She had not witnessed it personally, but she savored it as one of her most favorite moments in the recounting of Jesus' adventures: the day a sinful woman interrupted another dinner party Jesus attended. She walked right into the home of a Pharisee, brushed past all the men, knelt at Jesus' side, washed His feet with her tears, and anointed them with costly nard.

Suddenly, she knew what she had to do.

"Martha, I'll be right back," Mary called.

Mary ran home and went to the secret place where her most valuable treasure was stored. She reached on the top shelf and lifted the priceless jar of pure nard—a costly perfume. Mary had been saving it for her own wedding, but now she wanted to use it for her one true love. *I want to honor Jesus. He has welcomed me as a disciple, loved me like a sister, taught me as a student, and given my brother back to me from the grave. It is the least I can do. I know His time is short. I want to honor Him now.*

Beaming with anticipation, Mary ran back to Simon's home with passion and purpose. This time the disciples were not shocked at a woman's entrance into the room of men. After three years, they had grown accustomed to Jesus' welcoming ways.

Mary carefully moved through the room and hit her mark. She stopped where Jesus reclined at the table and knelt beside Him. With a snap, she broke the neck of the alabaster jar and poured its contents on Jesus' head and feet. Something stirred inside Mary as she anointed Jesus' body. A knowing.

Then Mary unbound her hair and wiped the excess from Jesus' calloused feet.

The sweet fragrance filled the room and clung to those nearby. Once they realized where the scent was coming from, a buzz of comments swarmed like the hum of bees. Some looked on with understanding and approval. Some turned up their noses in pious protest.

"What a waste," one of the disciples complained. "That perfume could have been sold at a high price and the money given to the poor."

Mary's heart sank at the unwelcome comment, but Jesus quickly buoyed her spirit with encouraging words. "Why are you bothering this woman?" He asked while placing His hand on her head. "She has done a beautiful thing to Me. You'll always have the poor to take care of, but you will not always have Me here with you. Don't you get it? When she poured this perfume on My body, she did it to prepare Me for burial. I tell you the truth," Jesus announced loud enough for all to hear, "wherever this gospel is preached throughout the world, what Mary has done will also be told."

Mary lifted her eyes to meet His and her heart spilled over with love.

A Closer Look

This account of Mary of Bethany anointing Jesus is recorded in three of the four Gospels: Matthew 26:6-13; Mark 14:3-9; John 12:1-8. We'll blend all three together to take a closer look. (Luke 7:37 also records an incident of a woman anointing Jesus at a dinner party, but this is clearly a different incident. The Luke account occurred at a Pharisee's home, and the woman honoring Jesus was referred to as a "sinful" woman.)

Six days before the Passover Jesus arrived at Bethany, where Lazarus lived, whom Jesus had raised from the dead. Here a dinner was given in Jesus' honor (John 12:1-2).

While Jesus was in Bethany in the home of a man known as Simon the Leper (Matthew 26:6).

The news of Lazarus' resurrection had added fuel to the fire of the Pharisees' determination to put Jesus to death. Jesus no doubt sensed the ominous cloud of death approaching, and while the partygoers celebrated with gaiety, Jesus contemplated the days ahead.

From the blending of these two passages, we learn that Jesus was at a dinner party in Simon the Leper's home. How would you like that name? "Sharon the Leper." But this is no ordinary leper. This is a healed leper. If he hadn't been healed, he would have been considered unclean and required to stand quite a distance from his guests, yelling "Unclean! Unclean!" Had he still been infected with this incurable disease, he might have had a dinner party, but he would have had few guests. A better name for this fellow would have been "Simon the Healed Leper."

Imagine the healed leper with skin as clear as a baby's bottom sharing a carafe of wine with the risen Lazarus. We can only imagine what other miracles gathered around the table.

The party was at Simon's home, but Martha and Mary were apparently the official hostesses for the event. Who better than Martha to be in charge of the details?

Martha served... (John 12:2).

No surprises here. Doesn't that just make you smile?

...while Lazarus was among those reclining at the table with him (John 12:2).

During dinner parties or banquets such as this one, guests did not sit at tables in chairs but reclined on floor cushions placed around the perimeter of low-lying tables. Their heads were near the table, while they leaned on one arm and ate with the other. So with His legs tucked behind Him, Jesus' feet would have been easily accessible.

> *Then Mary took about a pint of pure nard, an expensive perfume; she poured it on Jesus' feet and wiped his feet with her hair (John 12:3).*

Mark tells us that the perfume was contained in an alabaster jar (Mark 14:3). The jar was most likely a sealed flask with a long neck. Alabaster was a thin, delicate marble, and Mary could have easily broken the bottle's neck to pour out its fragrant contents.

Matthew and Mark recorded that she anointed Jesus' head; John noticed that she anointed His feet, but Jesus said, "She has anointed my body" (Matthew 26:12; Mark 14:8). While the disciples noticed the places the perfumed touched, Jesus pointed out the purpose. She wasn't merely anointing His head or his feet; she was preparing His body for burial.

According to B.F. Wescott, this was "the first stage in an embalming."[6] "One does not anoint the feet of a living person, but one might anoint the feet of a corpse as part of the ritual for preparing the whole body for burial."[7]

While the roar of dinner guests' laughter and chatter filled the room, I imagine Jesus' thoughts were elsewhere. A dark cloud was approaching. In only a few short days He would come face-to-face with evil and be crucified on a wooden cross. As the thoughts of what lay ahead loomed in Jesus' mind, in walked Mary. Mary had come not only to honor Jesus for who He was, but for what He would become—the supreme sacrifice.

Author Carolyn Custis James notes:

> While everyone else retreated and denied, even tried to set up road blocks to deter him from his mission, Mary came alongside and urged him forward. As darkness descended

over Bethany and the shadow of the cross fell across his path, she alone encouraged him to obey his Father. She alone said yes to the cross. It is a stunning moment, for Mary, and for us.[8]

Those closest to Jesus failed to understand Jesus' prediction of His death and resurrection. They were too busy arguing about who was the greatest among them and vying for the best seat in the heavenly kingdom. But Mary of Bethany understood and took action to prepare Jesus in the only way she could.

The nard was most likely Mary's dowry—for her future husband. When Mary let down her hair, this was also an act reserved for a woman's husband. How precious that Mary understood that Jesus was indeed her heavenly Bridegroom to whom she willingly gave her dowry and let down her hair.

She saw a need and met it. But I wonder if her actions and Jesus' response to it made the others in the room respond with, "Why didn't I think of that?" The same reaction took place when Jesus wrapped a towel around His waist and began washing His disciples' feet. "Here, let me do that," Peter said (John 13:1-17).

Oh, that we would be free to serve—to shed our hesitations and inhibitions. I never want to regret a missed opportunity and say, "Why didn't I think of that" when it comes to serving Jesus.

And the house was filled with the fragrance of the perfume
(John 12:3).

Not only did the fragrance fill the room, but everyone at the party carried the fragrance home with them. No doubt, the married men had some explaining to do when they arrived home.

The same thing happens when a woman worships Jesus today. She becomes the fragrance of Christ, and it clings to those around her.

But one of his disciples, Judas Iscariot, who was later to
betray him, objected. "Why wasn't this perfume sold and the
money given to the poor? It was worth a year's wages." He
did not say this because he cared about the poor but because

he was a thief; as keeper of the money bag, he used to help
himself to what was put into it (John 12:4-6).

Nard is fragrant oil made from the spikenard plant grown in northern India. As Judas pointed out, the amount that Mary used was worth a year's wages. He was not happy with her act of worship. It rubbed him the wrong way.

In Matthew's account of this story, it was after this dinner party that Judas went to the chief priests and offered to hand over Jesus for 30 pieces of silver. When someone has turned their back on God, nothing riles them more than a person who loves God with all her heart.

> Jesus said to them, "Why are you bothering this woman? She
> has done a beautiful thing to me. The poor you will always
> have with you, but you will not always have me. When she
> poured this perfume on my body, she did it to prepare me for
> burial" (Matthew 26:10-12).

It seems that Jesus always had to defend Mary. Whether it was taking up for her with her contentious sister or defending her in front of a group of burly men, Jesus respected Mary's choices and honored her actions.

Just a few days earlier, Jesus took the disciples aside and told them what was about to happen. "'We are going to Jerusalem,' he said, 'and the Son of Man will be betrayed to the chief priests and teachers of the law. They will condemn him to death and will hand him over to the Gentiles, who will mock him and spit on him, flog him and kill him. Three days later he will rise'" (Mark 10:33-34; see also Luke 18:31-33).

But the disciples did not get it. Perhaps they did not want to grasp the magnitude of Jesus' words or think of anything other than the idea that Jesus would be a victorious ruler over Jerusalem. Luke says that the truth was "hidden from them" (Luke 18:34). Perhaps God closed their eyes to the truth until the fulfillment had occurred. We aren't sure. Rather than grapple with the meaning of Jesus' words, the boys began arguing about who would have the best seat in the house of God's kingdom (Mark 10:35-44).

Through the years, many have viewed Mary's act as accidentally prophetic—as a sweet gesture. It is a mistake to think women in the Bible acted in powerful ways accidently—that they had no idea the significance their actions. I believe Mary knew exactly what she was doing. While others in the room appeared foggy in their understanding of Jesus' impending death, Mary seemed to have grasped its gravity. She appeared intentional in her actions. She knew what she was doing and why she was doing it. Jesus said as much: "She did this in preparation for my burial" (John 12:7 NLT). Mary the student was now Mary the teacher.

Just as Mary of Bethany's actions opened the door for women to learn and become disciples of the Word, her anointing of Jesus' feet opened the door for women to serve in ministry.

> *I tell you the truth, wherever this gospel is preached throughout the world, what she has done will also be told, in memory of her. (Matthew 26:13).*

There are few incidences in the New Testament where Jesus shone a spotlight on a particular person and said to everyone around, including you and me, "Take a look at this. This is important." Jesus took no chances that we would soon forget Mary of Bethany's prophetic actions and highlighted it for both then and now.

Freed from Others' Expectations

Mary had certain expectations placed on her by the culture... and by her sister. Her world didn't stray too far from the door frame of her home. She was expected to take care of the household duties and stay out of the affairs of men. That included the marketplace, the political arena, and the classrooms of the rabbis. Her world was very small.

I don't know if you have ever experienced the suffocating confinement of others' expectations on your life, but it is a very difficult burden to bear. Whether it is a woman shedding the expectations of her parents to become a physician and answering the call to the mission field, a young adult putting aside the expectations of peers to pull in the big salary in exchange for working at a nonprofit, a mother putting aside the expectations of a family steeped in public education and choosing to homeschool her children, a woman rejecting the expectations of her faith community to return to the workforce to support her financially struggling family, a woman walking away from expectations of coworkers and returning home to become a full-time mom, a missionary kid departing from the expectations of generations of missionaries to stay stateside and take a different path, or a woman resisting expectations of traditional roles to attend seminary and study theology…putting aside the expectations of others to do what God calls you to do can be difficult.

This is where we find Mary of Bethany. Society had certain expectations for Mary as a woman. Martha had certain expectations for Mary as a woman. The disciples had certain expectations for Mary as a woman. Would she dare loosen the chains of others' expectations and accept Jesus' invitation? Would she step out of the box that had defined her life?

When I think back through the men and women in the Bible who accomplished great feats for God, almost every one of them had to set aside the expectations of others to accept God's invitation to participate in His activity. Abraham had to set aside his father's expectations of carrying on the family business to answer God's call to become a nomad. Ruth had to set aside her family's expectations of staying in Moab to follow her mother-in-law and worship Jehovah—who to Ruth's family was a foreign god. Moses had to put aside his adoptive mother's expectations of becoming an Egyptian ruler to become Israel's deliverer. Peter, James, and John had to give up their fathers' expectations of running the family fishing business to follow Jesus. Jesus had to turn His back on His followers' expectations of becoming a political leader in order to fulfill God's purposes.

And here we are with Mary…a courageous woman who walked

away from the expectations of others and walked into Jesus' classroom. Jesus swung the door wide open. I'm so glad she chose to take her seat.

Freed to Accept God's Invitation

Carolyn had just entered seminary—a bastion of male religious training that had, until recently, posted a "No Girls Allowed" sign over its sacred doors. Oh, you wouldn't see the opposition to female students listed on the letterhead or posted over the entrance, but you might sense it in the eyes of the professors, the attitudes of the administrators, or the air of the registrars.

But Carolyn loved God's Word and wanted to study theology. It was important to her.

One professor, with more than a hint of mischief in his eyes, walked over to Carolyn as she pored over her theology books in the school library. "You know," he began, "there have never been any great women theologians."[9] His casual remark left its mark on Carolyn, and she began a journey to prove him wrong. Rather than discourage and dampen the enthusiasm of this 5'4" dynamo, the professor lit a fuse that released the power God had intended all along.

The professor was wrong. There have been many great women theologians and in this chapter, we met one of the first…Mary of Bethany.

Why are we taught? To keep knowledge to ourselves? I don't think so. That certainly wasn't Jesus' model in the New Testament. He taught His disciples so that they could in turn go out and teach others. Timothy wrote, "All Scripture is God-breathed and is useful for teaching, rebuking, correcting and training in righteousness so that [all God's people] may be thoroughly equipped for every good work" (2 Timothy 3:16-17). God's Word is not a secret treasure meant to be hoarded for our sole benefit. God's Word is discovered treasure meant to be invested into the lives of others.

John Wesley stated, "I learned more about Christianity from my mother than from all the theologians of England."

In the early part of the nineteenth century, God moved mightily through a preacher named Charles Finney. Finney often invited women to pray and speak in public gatherings. He started Oberlin College, which was the first college in America to allow women to study alongside men. He was the first Protestant leader to train women in theology. In 1853, Antoinette Brown, one of his former students, became the first woman ordained in America.[10]

Another great evangelical leader of the nineteenth century, Dwight L. Moody, was eager to educate women in theology. General William Booth used women in preaching and leadership roles throughout the Salvation Army.

Hannah Whithall Smith's book *The Christian's Secret to a Happy Life,* published in 1875, is still a well-loved classic for Christians all over the world. Her words have encouraged men and women alike in a closer walk with God, and it sits among my favorite volumes.

God calls women, right along with men, to be runners (Hebrews 12:1-2), warriors (Ephesians 6:10-18), ambassadors (2 Corinthians 5:20), teachers (Acts 18:26), prophets (Acts 2:17), and workers (Ephesians 2:10). And He calls us to be equipped by being students of His Word (2 Timothy 3:16-17).

As I sit at my computer, I am surrounded on every side with shelves filled with books written by men *and* women theologians. My heart swells with effervescent joy when I look at the titles penned by some of my dearest friends—sisters in Christ who accepted God's call on their lives to be taught by Him and then to teach others. Without their courage, I would most likely not be writing this book today.

We first met Mary as she walked into the classroom and became a student. But in our final scene, she turns the tables and teaches those around her. She didn't do it with her words, but with her actions. Jesus served as her interpreter and explained her prophetic message.

"She did what she could," Jesus told the disciples. Mary knew she was powerless to stop the evil that was about to be unleashed against Jesus. But she could do this. She could honor Him with what she had right now. She could prepare Him for burial before He faced the cross. Her tears let us know that she understood that the time for Him to die was near. This was not a celebratory offering. She was not joyful but mournful. Her actions were prophetic in the greatest sense.

Let's go back to Carolyn's seminary professor's comment. "You know, there have never been any great women theologians." Jesus would disagree. There have been many. He made sure of it. Mary of Bethany was one.

> *Wherever this gospel is preached throughout the whole world, what she has done will be told, in memory of her.*
>
> Matthew 26:13

9

The Stellar Student
(Martha of Bethany)

Freed from Worrisome Ways
Freed to Calm Confidence

J ust as with Mary of Bethany, we encounter her sister, Martha, in
three various scenes. We've already been a fly on the wall at two
dinner parties with Jesus, but now we need to rewind and look
at the stories from Martha's point of view. What was going on in
her mind? Was Jesus disappointed in Martha? How did Jesus' comment affect her in the long run? Let's rewind and join Martha in
the kitchen.

Steamed Up in the Kitchen

"So many details," Martha huffed as she ground wheat into a
fine powder. "That Lazarus. He's at it again. He just waltzes in here
and announces that Jesus and His friends are stopping by for dinner. Jesus! Not just anyone, but the prophet we've heard so much
about. The man who teaches with authority and heals with but a
word. Jesus!

"And a few friends? Count them. Twelve. A dinner party like this
takes days to prepare, and Lazarus gives me four hours' notice. There
is so much to do: mix the dough, let it rise, beat the dough, weave

the dough, cook the bread; prepare the lamb, roast the lamb, baste the lamb; select the wine, gather the goblets, pull the best plates from storage; sweep the floor, fluff the pillows, scrub the table; dust the furniture, fill the oil lamps, trim the wicks, polish the brass. My head is spinning just thinking of all the details."

"Who are you talking to?" Martha's sister, Mary, asked as she walked into the kitchen.

"I'm talking to myself," Martha answered. "I have much to do to prepare for Jesus' arrival, and I'm counting on you to do your part."

"Don't worry, Martha," Mary consoled. "Everything will be just fine."

Martha worked furiously, preparing all the details and barking out orders to anyone within earshot. And right in the middle of pounding the risen dough, she heard a knock at the door.

"Come on in," she heard her brother welcoming the guests. "We've been waiting for you!"

"Waiting my foot," Martha mumbled. "I'm working myself to death."

The men gathered in the front room, and soon Jesus captured their attention as He began teaching about the days to come and the kingdom of God.

"I'll take a bowl of fresh dates into the guests," Mary said. "That will give them something to nibble on while we finish the preparations."

"That's fine," Martha agreed. "But come right back."

Minutes passed, but Mary never returned to the kitchen. Finally, Martha peeked into the room and saw her sister sitting at Jesus' feet, taking in every word He said.

Martha angrily stomped into the gathering room with mixing bowl in hand. All eyes turned to the frustrated sister as she interrupted Jesus and pointed her wooden spoon in Mary's direction.

"Lord," she began sternly, "can't you see that Mary has left me all alone in the kitchen. What does she think she's doing? Don't You care that I have to do all this work by myself while my irresponsible sister is out here lollygagging about with the men. Why, she's not even supposed to be out here at all. It isn't proper for a woman to join a room full of men, much less sit at a rabbi's feet while he's teaching. Put her in her place! Tell her to get back in the kitchen where she belongs!"

"Martha, Martha," Jesus replied, "don't get so worked up. Mary is right where she needs to be. You are so worried, bothered, and distracted with the details of living that you miss the joys of life. You don't need to work so hard to create a feast for us. That's not even important. What *is* important is that I am here and have something to share with you. Mary has figured that out. She has chosen what is important and I am not going to send her away. She has joined the classroom to learn—to become a disciple of God's Word—and I am not going to take that away from her."

Martha put her flour-covered hand on her hip, spun around on her heels, and marched back into the kitchen. "Well, I never," she mumbled as she stomped away.

A Closer Look

We've taken a closer look at this story from Mary's point of view. Now let's see it from Martha's.

> As Jesus and his disciples were on their way, he came to a village where a woman named Martha opened her home to him. She had a sister called Mary, who sat at the Lord's feet listening to what he said. But Martha was distracted by all the preparations that had to be made. She came to him and asked, "Lord, don't you care that my sister has left me to do the work by myself? Tell her to help me!" (Luke 10:38-40).

Did you catch that Martha is telling Jesus what to do? She wants to be in control. Oh, I would never do that. Well...okay, maybe I have done that a time or two...or three. (How about you? Have you ever presumed to tell the all-knowing, all-powerful Creator of the universe what to do? If you have, check out God's response to a man who did the same. God's response is recorded in Job 38–41.)

*"Martha, Martha," the Lord answered, "you are worried and
upset about many things, but only one thing is needed. Mary
has chosen what is better, and it will not be taken away from
her" (Luke 10:41-42).*

The Greek word Jesus used here is translated "worried," but it can
also be translated "distracted." It literally means dragging all around, to
pull apart or to pull away. Another translation states that Martha was
"cumbered about much serving" (verse 40 KJV). "Cumbered" implies
"drawn away or distracted." The New American Standard Bible says,
"Martha, Martha, you are *worried* and *bothered* about so many things"
(verse 41). Finally, the Amplified Bible reads: "Martha, Martha, you
are *anxious* and *troubled* about many things; there is need of only one
or but a few things. Mary has chosen the good portion [that which is
to her advantage] which shall not be taken away from her" (verses 41-
42). Simply put, Martha was having a hissy fit about details.

I understand Martha's frustration. As I mentioned earlier, one
year I had 38 people for Thanksgiving dinner. If everyone had gathered around the television to watch the Thanksgiving parade while
I was left basting the turkey, stirring the gravy, mixing the stuffing,
baking the pumpkin pie, steaming the broccoli, and brewing the
tea, my emotions would have been basting, stirring, mixing, baking,
steaming, brewing as well. (That was not the case, by the way. Everyone pitched in, and all I had to do was make sure everyone had a
place to sit with their mounds of food.) But if we stop there, we are
missing the point. This section of Scripture is not about how Martha was feeling, but about what Jesus was inviting her to do.

Jesus didn't just wag His finger at Martha with a "tsk, tsk." No,
He used this as a teachable moment. "Martha, Martha," He began.
Don't you just love how He addressed her? With love and compas-
sion, He began to teach His lovely friend. His voice didn't have a
hint of anger. In effect, He was inviting Martha to become one is
His students as well.

Jesus used this teachable moment for Mary, for Martha, and for
the disciples. He also used it for me and for you, fellow students

who would enter into His classroom in the years to come. He always takes advantage of the teachable moments when the soil is well tilled and waiting to receive the seed.

Jesus' response was certainly not what Martha expected, or she wouldn't have voiced her irritation in the first place. I imagine she thought Jesus would have quickly sided with her and pointed Mary back to the kitchen where she belonged. His response wasn't what the disciples expected, either. After all, women were not supposed to be learning with the men but cooking with the women. However, Jesus seldom responded as they expected. He surprised them all. He opened the way for women to come into His classroom and sit in the front row with ready hearts and minds.

Jesus loved Martha and invited her to join Him in the classroom. He put a lid on her boiling emotions and left her to simmer on what He had just said. Ever wonder what happened next? Let's take a look at the second scene to get a clue.

Called Up to Profess Her Faith

It's easy to fall into the trap of thinking of Martha and Mary as mere characters in a story, but they were real women just like you and me. They had daily trials and triumphs, past regrets and remorse, and future hopes and dreams. Yet even though we share many similarities, their living conditions were very different. Single women in those days, whether never married or widowed, depended on their brothers or fathers to take care of them. They didn't usually work outside the home and there was no welfare system to take care of the disenfranchised. Retirement plan? That would be a brother or son. For these two women, Lazarus was all they had. If he died, their future died with him. In our second encounter with the sisters, that is the very cliff upon which their future teeters. Let's join them now, not in the dining room hosting a party, but in the sickroom fearing for their brother's life.

"Martha," Mary cried, "What are we going to do? We've tried

everything, and yet Lazarus' skin is still so hot. Even cold water fails to lower his fiery fever. His eyes are glazed, his tongue is like pale parchment, and he no longer responds to our voices."

Martha thought about her strong brother. He never got sick. But this sickness had come over him so quickly, and nothing they did seemed to help. His body burned with fever and only cooled temporarily when bathed in the cool well water. He hadn't eaten for days and only drank when she could force him to take a few unwanted sips.

"We have only one hope," Martha decided. "Someone needs to go and get Jesus. He could heal him with but a word."

"That's it!" Mary cried. "I'll send someone right away!"

Martha sighed and nodded.

"Daniel," Mary called to a trusted friend who paced in the yard waiting for word of his friend's health. "Go get Jesus. We need Him right away. Last I heard He was teaching by the Jordan."

"What shall I tell Him?" Daniel asked.

"Tell Him, 'The one You love is sick,'" she replied. "He'll know what to do."

So off Daniel ran to find the Master. But only moments after he left Bethany, Lazarus took a turn for the worse and breathed his last.

When Daniel arrived and gave Jesus the news, the Teacher did not respond as the messenger had expected. Even His disciples were surprised by His seeming lack of concern. "This sickness is not the end of Lazarus. It's actually a way for God and His Son to be glorified," Jesus replied. The disciples didn't understand many of Jesus' statements, and this response was certainly one of them.

Jesus didn't pick up and go to His friend right away. Rather, He stayed at the camp for two more days, waiting for His heavenly Father's directions. Then, on the third day, God signaled it was time to go.

It took one day for Daniel to reach Jesus, two days for God to give Jesus the signal to leave, and one more day for Him to finally arrive in Bethany. By the time Jesus reached the city limits, Lazarus had been dead four days and his body was securely sealed away in the cavelike tomb.

A crowd gathered at Martha and Mary's home to grieve their loss. When Martha heard that Jesus was only a short distance away, she ran to meet Him.

"Lord," Martha cried as she fell at Jesus' feet, "if You had been here, this would not have happened. Lazarus would not have died. Where were You? Why didn't You come?"

Even as the accusing words spilled from Martha's mouth, she felt ashamed. Quickly she tried to cover her ill-spoken remarks. "But I know that even now God will give You whatever You ask."

Jesus placed His hand on Martha's shoulder and quietly spoke. "Your brother will rise again."

"I know he will rise again in the resurrection at the last day," she responded.

Jesus continued, "I am the resurrection and the life. If anyone believes in Me, he will live, even if he dies. Martha, do you believe this?"

"I do, Lord," she replied. "I believe that You are the Son of God, whose coming was promised to us."

Jesus' heart soared with pride at Martha's words. While so many of His closest friends didn't understand who He was and what He came to do, this student saw it clearly. She passed the test with flying colors and moved to the head of the class. Oh, how He loved her!

"Martha, go and get Mary for Me. I want to talk to her too."

Martha ran back to the house full of wailing mourners and whispered in Mary's ear. "Jesus is here. He's asking for you."

Mary leapt to her feet and rushed out the door. Many of the mourners thought Mary was running to the tomb in a surge of grief and followed after her. When she arrived at the place where Jesus waited, she too fell at His feet. "Oh Lord, if You had been here, my brother would not have died. Why didn't You come? Where have You been?"

When Jesus saw her broken heart, tears filled His eyes. Oh, how He hated death. How He loathed the result of sin and Satan's sting. He was so overcome with emotion and love for this family that he couldn't even offer a word of condolence.

"Where have you laid him?" Jesus asked.

"Come and see," she replied.

When Jesus arrived at the tomb, He couldn't contain His emotions any longer. He wept. Salty tears fell from the face of God-made-man and spilled on the cursed ground.

Jesus surveyed the crowd and caught the eye of two strapping young men. "Take the stone away from the mouth of the cave," He instructed them.

"But, Lord," Martha said, "Lazarus has been in the tomb for four days. His body will have started to decay. There will be a terrible stench."

"Martha, trust Me. Didn't I tell you that if you believed you would see the glory of God?" He replied.

So the men rolled away the stone as the crowd held their breath in anticipation.

Jesus prayed aloud and then called out in a loud voice toward the tomb. "Lazarus, come out!"

Silence hung in the air like a low-lying cloud. And then…and then…a linen-bound man stiffly appeared from the mouth of the cave and into the welcoming light of day.

Gasps, cheers, and cries of joy filled the air.

"Unbind him and let him go," Jesus instructed.

A Closer Look

You know what? Reading and retelling that story makes me tired. I have so many emotions going up and down and left and right with the sisters—I'm just exhausted.

Have you ever sat by someone's bedside and watched his or her life slip away? It is a helpless feeling. There is nothing you can do as the body begins to shut down like the lights going out in a tall building. I am sure the sisters did everything they knew to do, and yet nothing helped.

I have never felt that more clearly than when my father-in-law died in 2008. His health had been declining, but with no diagnosis that would eventually take his life. He was simply ebbing away from us, and there was nothing we could do. Then one morning he simply stopped breathing...he left us. He was gone.

And while we mourned our loss and celebrated his heavenly gain, it was Mary Ellen, his wife of 64 years, who could not move past her grief. No one—not her four children, five grandchildren, or five great-grandchildren—could abate her fathomless sadness. Again, we felt powerless as we watched her begin to slip away and the lights go out in her life as well. Six months after my father-in-law died, his precious wife had a sudden heart attack and joined him in eternity. When death comes knocking, we humans are powerless to stop its intrusion. But Jesus was about to show that He is master over life and death.

Much had happened since Jesus' initial visit in Martha's home. He had opened the eyes of the blind, made the lame to walk, cleansed the lepers' skin, multiplied the bread, and raised the dead. The small village of Bethany would have received reports of Jesus' teachings and miracles. No matter what the masses thought about who He was—they could not deny what He did.

Martha didn't just hear *about* Jesus. She heard *from* Jesus. Now her friendship and faith were being tested. She knew Him as teacher, healer, and friend. Now He was taking her to a deeper level of understanding. He wanted her to understand that He was the Lord of life and death, and sovereign King of all.

Let's take a closer look at the story as told by John.

> *Now a man named Lazarus was sick. He was from Bethany,*
> *the village of Mary and her sister Martha. This Mary, whose*
> *brother Lazarus now lay sick, was the same one who poured*
> *perfume on the Lord and wiped his feet with her hair (John*
> *11:1-2).*

Interestingly, when we met Martha and Mary in our first encounter, there was no mention of their brother, Lazarus. But as the story unfolds, we learn that he was one of Jesus' dearest friends.

In this passage, John mentioned Mary pouring perfume on Jesus' feet. However, this had not happened yet. This didn't happen until the week of Jesus' death and resurrection. Here, John gives us a taste of what is yet to come.

> So the sisters sent word to Jesus, "Lord, the one you love is sick" *(John 11:3).*

John, the disciple who penned this account, often referred to himself as "the one Jesus loved." But here, the sisters refer to their brother in those same endearing terms.

Martha didn't presume to tell Jesus what to do as she did in their kitchen encounter. She simply explained the situation and trusted Jesus to take care of it as He saw best. When it came to healing her brother, she didn't care how He did it, just that He did. Boy, was she in for a surprise—which is often the case when we leave matters in God's hands to work in the way He chooses, unhindered by our own interference.

If Martha had had a watch, you can believe she would have checked it often. "Where is He?" she must have wondered. "What's taking so long?" Her hope was ebbing away with her brother's waning life.

> When he heard this, Jesus said, "This sickness will not end in death. No, it is for God's glory so that God's Son may be glorified through it" *(John 11:4).*

This statement is reminiscent of Jesus' explanation to His disciples as to why a certain man was born blind:

> As he went along, he saw a man blind from birth. His disciples asked him, "Rabbi, who sinned, this man or his parents, that he was born blind?" "Neither this man nor his parents sinned," said Jesus, "but this happened so that the work of God might be displayed in his life" (John 9:1-3).

Oh, that we would have the same attitude when difficulties come our way. "Dear God, I know that You will be glorified in this circumstance. I don't understand what is happening or why, but I know that You will work it out for my good and for the good of those who are watching my story unfold. I pray that many will believe in You because of what You will do and that they will see Your glory."

Now Jesus loved Martha and her sister and Lazarus (John 11:5).

Hold everything! This is one of my favorite passages in the entire story. See, for so many years, Martha has gotten a bad rap. Mary has been portrayed as the lovely lady who sat pensively at Jesus' feet and Martha as the grumpy sister bossing everyone around. In our skewed imaginations, we picture Jesus loving Mary and disapproving of Martha. But read that verse again. "Now Jesus loved Martha and old what's her name." I love it! Not because I am *not* a fan of Mary, but because I *am* a fan of Martha. I'm crazy about her, just like Jesus was. Let's keep going and I'll tell you why in a moment.

> *Yet when he heard that Lazarus was sick, he stayed where he was two more days. Then he said to his disciples, "Let us go back to Judea" (John 11:6-7).*

When John used the word "yet," it was as if he were saying, *I just didn't get it. He loved them, but He waited. What's up with that? If He would stop to help a stranger, certainly He would travel to heal a friend.*

Jesus didn't go at once because God had a greater plan. It would have been a miracle on a small scale to heal a sick friend, but it would be a miracle on a grand scale to raise him from the dead. It is a difficult lesson to wait on God when degenerating circumstances are draining our hope dry, but God wants to make sure we understand that we are absolutely helpless in our own strength so that we will understand the greatness of His.

Two days later, God gave the signal. It was time to go.

Not only was it time to go and perform the miraculous resurrection of Lazarus that we know is on the way, it was also time for Jesus to return to the very area where the Pharisees were seeking to kill Him. There was clear and present danger in His decision to return to Judea. The Pharisees had already tried to stone Him, and Jesus knew they were plotting His death. He also knew they were going to succeed. And…it was time. The end was drawing near, and this monumental miracle would make the Pharisees more determined than ever to kill Him.

The disciples warned Jesus not to go back into hostile territory, but Jesus was firm in His resolve. Jesus further confused their thinking by explaining that Lazarus was already dead. To the disciples, traveling to Bethany did not seem like a wise career move. They didn't see the point. Lazarus was already dead, so why take the chance? To Jesus, it was the next step to accomplishing His ultimate goal.

By the time Jesus arrived, Lazarus' decaying body had been in the tomb for four days. Jewish tradition called for 30 days of mourning, and the wailing was in full swing. This death shook the entire village, and many Jews from surrounding cities came to mourn the loss. For these two women, it was more than the loss of a brother. With no husband, no children, no father, and now no brother, they were left with no one to take care of them in a culture where it was difficult for a woman to provide for her own needs.

> When Martha heard that Jesus was coming, she went out to meet him, but Mary stayed at home. "Lord," Martha said to Jesus, "if you had been here, my brother would not have died" (John 11:20-21).

Have you ever felt the same way? *Lord, if You had been here, this would not have happened. Where were You? Where are You now?* Martha was disappointed in Jesus—He could have prevented Lazarus' death. But as always, Jesus wasn't late. He was right on time.

Martha's internal battle between the realities of her brother's decaying body and the knowledge that Jesus could have prevented it battled for supremacy. She's no different than you and me. We often have the same battle of the mind when faith and tragedy collide.

The truth is, God was there! He is omnipresent—everywhere all at once. Even in the stairwell of the Twin Towers as they crumbled to the ground? Even there. Even in a shanty swept away by hurricane Katrina? Even there. Even when I looked at the ultrasound of my baby and discovered no heartbeat? Even there.

Do you think that Jesus knew Mary and Martha would be disappointed in Him for not showing up before Lazarus died? Of course He did. But nevertheless, He waited. He waited because He was more interested in glorifying God than a quick fix with little impact.

Martha spoke what was on her heart, but then as quickly as the words escaped her weary lips, she wanted to take them back.

> *But I know that even now God will give you whatever you ask" (John 11:22).*

It was an "oops" moment. What had been rambling around in her head tumbled out of her mouth. Martha quickly backpedaled and spoke what she *knew* to be true in her head, even though she didn't *feel* it to be true in her heart. She knew Jesus could, even now, raise Lazarus from the dead. He *could* do anything.

> *Jesus said to her, "Your brother will rise again." Martha answered, "I know he will rise again in the resurrection at the last day." Jesus said to her, "I am the resurrection and the life. He who believes in me will live, even though he dies; and whoever lives and believes in me will never die. Do you believe this?" (John 11:23-26).*

Do you see what Jesus is doing here? He is teaching Martha the fundamental principles of the gospel: Belief in Jesus leads to eternal life with God. While the disciples were standing by, Jesus was teaching a woman. This is why I love Martha. She did indeed leave the kitchen and join Jesus in the classroom. She did put aside her worrisome ways, her distracting details, and her bossy behavior. After she simmered down, Martha accepted Jesus' invitation to become a disciple in her own right. She became a stellar student and moved to the head of the class with Mary.

Jesus didn't tell Martha to buck up and take it like a man. Once again, He tenderly took advantage of a teachable moment and took her to a place of deeper understanding. "He uses our struggles to help us realize we don't know him nearly as well as we think we do and to draw us closer to him."[1] In usual Jesus-style, He did so by asking questions…"Do you believe this?"

This was Martha's pop quiz. Let's see if she passed.

> *"Yes, Lord," she told him, "I believe that you are the Christ, the Son of God, who was to come into the world" (John 11:27).*

Martha understood. Her profession of faith during a time when even Jesus' closest friends were unsure is remarkable. She was a magnificent woman of faith who had learned her lessons well. This is why I am a Martha fan. Her response is very telling. Her words let us know that she did choose what was better and joined her sister at the feet of the Teacher.

During difficulties, God puts our beliefs in a sifter to grind out the lumps of doubt that perhaps we didn't even know existed. Struggles test our faith and solidify our beliefs. As Peter wrote, trials come so that our faith "may be proved genuine" (1 Peter 1:7). Martha's theology was solid. She knew what she believed.

Now Jesus was about to reveal an even deeper truth. He is sovereign over life and death, and our time constrictions are irrelevant to the Creator of time itself.

> *And after she had said this, she went back and called her sister Mary aside. "The Teacher is here," she said, "and is asking for you" (John 11:28).*

The words, "Jesus is asking for you," give me chills. Can you imagine someone knocking on your door with the same invitation? "Jesus is asking for you." The truth is, God *does* knock on the door, and Jesus *is* asking for you, Jesus wants *you* to come to Him. "Come to me, all you who are weary and burdened, and I will give you rest" (Matthew 11:28).

In the Garden of Eden, after Adam and Eve hid from God because of their sin, God walked into their shame and asked, "Where are you?" (Genesis 3:9). He called them out of hiding. No matter what they had done, He still longed for a relationship with His image bearers. He longs for a relationship with you. He is asking for you.

When Mary ran to meet Jesus and fell at His feet, He was so moved He couldn't even offer any words of consolation. He simply asked, "Where have you laid him?" And what happened when Jesus arrived at the tomb surrounded by mourners? Two simple words:

Jesus wept (John 11:35).

The mourners' pain opened a floodgate of emotion in Jesus. He understood Martha and Mary's hurt...and He understands ours as well.

We know the rest of the story. Jesus did indeed raise Lazarus from the dead and many people put their faith in Him as a result. However, there were some who did not welcome the miracle. Rather, they ran to the Pharisees and gave them more ammunition to crucify Him (John 11:46). Isn't that always the case? We will either choose to believe or run in the opposite direction.

Martha had learned a great deal on her field trip of faith. We don't know for sure, but I imagine after her brother's resurrection, she fell at Jesus' feet once again.

Freed from Worrisome Ways

For centuries Martha has been used in sermons as an example of what not to be. "Too busy for Jesus?" the preacher asks. "Don't be a Martha," the teacher warns. "Be a Mary."

We have a tendency to ask, "Are you a Mary or a Martha" as if we have to choose. Just yesterday I told a friend I was currently writing about Martha. "Oh, I'm definitely a Martha," she replied.

"No, you're not," I responded. "You're a Jennifer."

We tend to categorize women (including ourselves) into "thinkers" or "doers," as if the two cannot coexist. We label ourselves, and others, as worshippers or workers, when the truth is we must be both.

Not for a minute do I believe that Martha stayed in the kitchen forever. Not for a minute do I believe that Mary stayed out of it. By Martha's confession of faith after Lazarus' death, we see that she had joined Mary at the feet of Rabbi Jesus. She didn't become *just* a student. She moved to the top of the class.

We also tend to read the story of Mary and Martha and see one student. Jesus saw two. He took the opportunity to teach Martha right where she was. Sometimes we go to Him to learn and sometimes He comes to us. He interrupts our hissy fits and says, "Hey, wait a minute, sister. Let's look at this situation together."

Can I broach another sensitive subject? Jesus let Martha know that there were more important things in life than taking care of the cooking and cleaning.

Now, before you think I'm saying get a maid and read your Bible all day long, you need to know that I love taking care of my home. Each time I finish writing a book, I take a month off and tackle a big decorating project. I make curtains, paint murals, sew pillows, or reupholster furniture. But as much as I enjoy the busyness of creating and maintaining a lovely home, God reminds me that the most important activity of each and every day are the moments I spend in communion with Him.

Jesus never talked down to Martha but gently instructed her. Again, He completely reversed the traditional priorities outlined for women of that day and invited her to become a disciple—a student of God's Word. While the culture dictated that women were exempt from learning the Torah, Jesus showed her that learning about God was the best choice of all.

Freed to Calm Confidence

What do you think Martha did after she walked back into the kitchen? We are not told. Luke simply goes on to another story and leaves us with Martha holding the spoon and Jesus holding the door.

M.L. del Mastro, in his book *All the Women of the Bible*, retells stories of biblical women in narratives that paint beautiful land-scapes with the simple outlines given in the Scriptures. In his story of Martha, he writes that Martha was freed from "the imprisoning, lethal order she craved, so that she could live."[2] He went on to say:

> After that amazing meal, order gradually became less and less her god, less the air she needed for breathing, and more simply a product of her active giving and receiving of love. She learned to relax and let other people do what they did best without feeling challenged or threatened, because she learned that she could be, was in fact, loved for who she was, not for what she did and how she did it. That was how her service was becoming service in reality, not just a disguise for control nor a means to prevent her own annihilation. That "better part" became her choice as well, thanks to Him.[3]

Have you ever wondered why the story of Martha steamed up in the kitchen was included in Luke's Gospel in the first place? It's not about a healing, deliverance, or absolution of sin. It is not one of Jesus' parables or related to His journey to the cross. Think about it. I believe the story is included as an example of how Jesus came to set women free...free to become His disciples, to sit at His feet, and to join the classroom that had previously been reserved for men. I believe it is included to help women see just what is truly impor-tant in this life.

So what did Martha do after she walked back in the kitchen? I'll tell you what I think she did. I think she stewed a bit more—maybe for the rest of the day. But at some point Martha took Jesus up on His invitation to join Him in the classroom. She became a disciple as well. How do I know? Because of her response to Jesus' pop quiz after Lazarus died. "I believe that you are the Christ, the Son of God, who was to come into the world," she replied. Yes, she passed with flying colors.

Our last glimpse of Martha is at Simon the Leper's dinner party, where Mary anointed Jesus' body with perfume and prepared Him for burial. And where is Martha? Why, she's in the kitchen serving. Being a disciple of Jesus Christ does not release us from our day-to-day activities and responsibilities. We still cook dinner, vacuum the house, dust the furniture, go to the office, drive carpool, and fold laundry. But knowing Jesus gives us the freedom to serve joyfully, giving to others out of the overflow of our relationship with the Savior. God didn't change her natural bent toward serving, but He did change her sinful bent toward complaining, projecting her expectations, and attempting to control others.

Yes, at this final party, Martha was serving in the kitchen. She wasn't fussing about it, worried, bothered, and distracted because Mary wasn't doing her part. After all, Mary was right where she belonged. This time Martha served with a new attitude of thanksgiving and praise for the One who had set her free.

She was free to be who God has created her to be...Martha.

Jesus loved Martha and her sister and Lazarus.

JOHN 11:5

10

THE BENT BUT BRAVE

Freed from a Crippled Spirit
Freed to Walk in Confidence

t was another Sabbath day, much like any other. But as Mariah opened her eyes she had no idea this would be the day that changed her life.

"I'm getting too old for this," Mariah groaned as she twisted her crooked body to roll her stiff frame out of bed. "I wish I could just stay home today, but it is the Sabbath."

She swung her legs over the edge of the bed and dropped her feet onto the cold, hard floor. Her gaze and feet hit the packed dirt surface simultaneously, where both spent their waking hours.

"At least in bed I can see the sky through the window, the bird on its perch, and the faces of those I love," she moaned. "But even an old woman like myself can't stay in bed all day."

As Mariah stood, if you can call it that, she was in for another day of looking down at the dirt-packed floor, dusty gravel roads, and the mud-caked feet of passersby. For 18 years she had been crippled, bent over by an evil spirit that taunted her day and night. Her infirmity hadn't happened all at once, but progressed gradually, as if someone were laying bricks on the back of her neck, one by one, day by day. Her back began to slowly succumb to the invisible weight and bend like a bruised reed. Now her spine was parallel to the floor, and a hump remained where a young girl's strong back had been.

"I am so tired of looking at feet," she moaned, "but at least I can see. I can hear. I can speak. I have much to be thankful for. So today I will go to the synagogue to worship."

Mariah ran a comb through her gnarled gray hair, covered her head with a veil, and slipped sandals on her wrinkled feet. Then her shuffle to the temple began. Her frame prohibited her from looking up to find the women's section of the synagogue, so she just followed the feminine feet to find her seat…in the back and at the bottom of the temple's progressive tiers.

She couldn't see His face, but she knew that the person who stood to speak was not the usual teacher of the law. As soon as He approached the podium, whispers stirred like a hive of bees. "It's Jesus," they began. "The teacher and healer everyone is talking about." "It's Jesus! It's Jesus!"

Ignoring the buzz, Jesus began to teach. Unlike any other man she had ever heard before, Jesus spoke with authority and compassion. For the first time in her life, someone explained the Scriptures in a way that made sense to her. He explained spiritual truths with everyday examples that made His teaching come alive.

Oh, I wish I could see His face, she silently prayed.

No sooner had the words raced across her mind than Jesus stopped. She could not see Him, but He could see her.

A hush fell over the room.

"Woman, come forward," He instructed.

Mariah strained to lean back on her bench in order to see whom He was speaking to. "He's talking to *you*," her neighbor whispered. "He's looking right at you."

Mariah wasn't exactly sure what she should do. Jesus was asking her to leave the women's section of the synagogue and walk up the steps that separated the women from the men. He was calling her into forbidden territory. After a few moments of internal struggle, faith overcame fear and Mariah was out of her seat. She couldn't see their faces, but she knew all eyes were on her slow dragging gait forward.

Women gasped at her courage. Men glared at her audacity. Both parted as Mariah passed through.

After many long moments of painful struggle, Mariah finally arrived at the front of the crowd—center stage. Jesus bent down, placed His hand on the mountain that had become Mariah's back and leveled the land. She felt warmth surge through her frozen muscles as years of stiffness melted away. Like a marionette in the hands of a puppeteer, Jesus pulled her up. For the first time in 18 years, her crooked spine stood like a tall cedar. The physical malady that had defined her was gone, and she rose to look into the eyes of the One who had set her free.

"Woman," He spoke, "you are free from your infirmity."

Tears of joy coursed down her weathered cheeks, and the words of the psalmist coursed through her veins. "But thou, O LORD, art a shield for me; my glory, and the lifter up of mine head."[1]

"Thank You, Jesus!" she cried. "Thank You, Jesus!" She twirled around and raised her hands in praise to God. She laughed with lightness, and others rejoiced with her. No longer did she feel like the dirt she was forced to stare at day in and day out. She was free!

A Closer Look

Let me tell you why I love this story. I love it because, while I can't relate to being physically crippled for 18 years, I can relate to being emotionally crippled for the same amount of time. Being crippled comes in many forms. We'll get to that in just a moment, but for now, let's take a closer look at one dear sister who was set free to dance again.

> *On a Sabbath Jesus was teaching in one of the synagogues...*
> *(Luke 13:10).*

I almost hold my breath when a story begins with the words "It was the Sabbath." I know right away that Jesus is about to ruffle some feathers. He constantly broke through the binding barriers of the who, what, when, and where that the religious leaders had set in place. In this first sentence, we get a hint that Jesus is about to ignore a "when." It was the Sabbath and He was up to something.

> *...and a woman was there who had been crippled by a spirit for eighteen years. She was bent over and could not straighten up at all (Luke 13:11).*

Now Luke tells us the "who." A woman. Barrier number two.

> *When Jesus saw her, he called her forward...(Luke 13:12).*

Herod's Temple stood on a hill overlooking the beautiful city of Jerusalem. It was built by Herod and his sons between 19 BC–63 AD. While most of it was completed by 9 BC, adornment continued for 72 more years. The structure reflected the religious and societal prejudices of the day, with ascending sets of steps and partitions to separate various people groups. The outer area, the court of the Gentiles, was a general area open to all Jews and God-fearing Gentiles. The next level up was called the court of women, where both Jewish men and women were welcomed. The third tier was called the court of the Israelites, and only ceremonially clean Jewish men were allowed. The fourth set of steps led to the Holy Place, where only the priests could enter. Finally, the fifth level contained the Most Holy Place, where the High Priest entered once a year, on the Day of Atonement. A heavy embroidered curtain hung in front of the Most Holy Place and separated man from the presence of God.[2]

In the Old Testament, the God-designed tabernacle had only three divisions. The outer court for all, the Holy Place for the appointed priests, and the Holy of Holies, where only the high priest could enter once a year. According to Deuteronomy 31:12 and Joshua 8:35, all people, both men and women, were encouraged to attend regular readings of the Law. The divisions we see in Herod's Temple during the time of Christ were not God ordained, but man-made based on prejudice.

The woman with the crippled back was in the court of women, and while this may not have been in Herod's Temple in Jerusalem, other synagogues were set up much the same way. She would have been seated at the back, where the women always gathered. A dividing curtain or partition and a set of steps separated the women from the men, and "No Girls Allowed" was understood by all.

As one commentator noted: "Jesus' invitation to the crippled woman struck out against the male monopoly of public worship. When Jesus put her in the spotlight, right down in front of the whole synagogue, He shattered the men's worldview. There must have been a collective gasp from dignified rows of men that day. Didn't Jesus know what He was doing? Women were supposed to be kept in their place, hidden behind the dividing screens!"[3]

Now Luke tells us the "where." Barrier number three. Jesus called the woman out of the shadows of the women's section and onto center stage. And, finally, the "what." Then she was healed.

Yes, Jesus knew the man-made rules, and the God-made-man ignored them. Once again, He refused to be governed by the religious rulers' false sense of propriety and stayed the course of setting men *and* women free.

> *"Woman, you are set free from your infirmity." Then he put his hands on her, and immediately she straightened up and praised God (Luke 13:12-13).*

Just like that?

Just like that.

This is one incident when Jesus did not mention the woman's faith. In the case of the woman with the 12-year bleeding, Jesus said, "Daughter, your faith has healed you" (Mark 5:34). However, in this case the woman's faith wasn't mentioned. But make no mistake about it, there was faith involved. In order for her to receive healing, she had to take a step of faith...several steps, actually. And where those steps took her was enough to make any women quake in her sandals.

> *Indignant because Jesus had healed on the Sabbath, the synagogue ruler said to the people, "There are six days for*

work. So come and be healed on those days, not on the
Sabbath" (Luke 13:14).

Not everyone was happy about Jesus miraculously healing this crippled woman. The *who, what, when,* and *where* of the healing riled the ruler. He was more concerned with the binding law than the bound-up woman. This healing was not on the schedule or in the bulletin, so to speak. It was out of order—their order.

The synagogue ruler? Wait a minute. Who is that guy?

> A ruler of the synagogue was a layman whose responsibili-
> ties were administrative and included such things as look-
> ing after the building and supervising worship. Though
> there were exceptions, most synagogues had only one ruler.
> Sometimes the title was honorary, with no administrative
> responsibilities assigned.[4]

So the synagogue ruler was a volunteer bouncer. He made sure that everything was done in order and according to the book. *Which* book and *whose* book are somewhat debatable.

Interestingly, when the synagogue ruler made his statement of chastisement, he made it to the people, not to Jesus. He turned around and addressed the crowd. "Listen folks. Strike this miracle from the record. Church is no place for healing. You can get healed on Sunday through Friday, but not on Saturday. We are here to worship, not get healed." (Their Sabbath was on our Saturday.)

Imagine this scenario. Imagine you are in church. Right in the middle of the sermon, the pastor steps away from the podium and motions for a man in a wheelchair to come forward. The man slowly rolls the chair down the aisle and stops at the edge of the platform.

Then the pastor looks the man in the eye and says, "Harry, God is healing you today. You are free from your wheelchair. Get up and walk." As the man rises, for the first time in 18 years, the congregation breaks out in wild applause laced with tears and praises to God.

But then an elder runs forward and addresses the congregation.

"Hold everything!" he begins. "This healing is not on the schedule today. It is not printed here in the bulletin. This is not the time and place for healings, Harry. You'll have to come back next week and we'll write you in."

How crazy would that be! And yet that is the same feeling we get when the synagogue ruler condemns Jesus' actions to the crowd. Because of his sour attitude, he missed the joy of the miracle. As a result, he also missed true worship because of his dogged determination to follow man-made rules.

Interestingly, the ruler called the act of healing "work." Work? Did he really call it work? This kind of miracle takes a work of God, but all we have to do is believe and receive. Jesus didn't work up a sweat. Actually, healing is a piece of cake for Him.

> *The Lord answered him, "You hypocrites! Doesn't each of you on the Sabbath untie his ox or donkey from the stall and lead it out to give it water? Then should not this women, a daughter of Abraham, whom Satan has kept bound for eighteen long years, be set free on the Sabbath day from what bound her?" (Luke 13:15-16).*

The synagogue ruler spoke to the people, but Jesus answered directly to him. He made a direct correlation between a bound animal and the bound woman.

As I mentioned earlier, Jesus was very intentional in the who, what, when, and where of His miracles. It was no accident that this occurred on the Sabbath. Jesus demonstrated that relationship was more important than religion, people were more important than platitudes, and receptive hearts were more important than repetitive ritual.

If a donkey could be unbound on the Sabbath, how much more could a daughter of Abraham be unbound from her infirmity? Did the ruler think animals were more important than people? That is a good question for us to consider. In a culture that treats pets better than some people, we certainly hold some upside-down views on the importance of life created in God's image and the creation made for us to enjoy. But from the response of the temple ruler, this is nothing new.

Jesus said something precious about this woman. He called her a "daughter of Abraham." Nowhere in the Old Testament do we find such words. Several men were referred to as "sons of Abraham," but not until the Liberator comes do we see the same words of endearment and honor used to refer to women.

"I think there was another reason the woman stood straight and tall that day in the synagogue. Jesus had done more than heal her back. He had restored her dignity as a person, showing her that she was valued by God. She was an equal heir with her male counterparts to all that God had promised Abraham."[5]

Eighteen years? Who told Jesus she had been crippled for 18 years? I don't see that anywhere in the text. Could it be that Jesus knew that bit of information because He knew every day of her life? Could it be He knew the days that were marked out for her, the days she would be crippled, and the day she would be set free? I believe so.

> When he said this, all his opponents were humiliated, but the people were delighted with all the wonderful things he was doing (Luke 13:17).

Some praised God for what Jesus had done. Others turned up their pious noses. But she didn't care what anyone thought. She was healed.

And you know what? Jesus didn't care what anyone thought, either.

Once there was a woman who was bound...and there was a Healer who was bound to set her free. No longer would she be known as "the woman with the crippled back." Now she would be known as "the woman Jesus healed."

Freed from a Crippled Spirit

I was riding down the crowded streets of Mexico City in a cab when I saw her. She measured about four feet high, back curved and bent at the waist at a 90-degree angle, fingers gnarled and twisted shut. Like an upside-down chair, her face was parallel to the dirty sidewalk. Feet, dirt, trash. That was her view of the world. She shuffled alongside our car as we inched through congested traffic. I saw her, but she did not see me. She could not see me. She just saw feet.

Sharon, look at My daughter, God seemed to say. *When you read about the woman with the crippled back, never again see her as a character in a story. See her as you see this woman now. Flesh and blood. Real and relevant. My daughter. Your sister.*

God reminded me once again that these women we read about in the Bible were real people just like you and me. We must never forget that. And while we might not be able to relate to being crippled physically, most of us can relate to being crippled emotionally. We see feet—people passing by going about their busy lives. We see dirt—the mistakes we've made through the years. We see trash—the pain inflicted on us by others and many times by our own poor decisions.

Jesus said, "Come to me, all you who are weary and burdened, and I will give you rest. Take my yoke upon you and learn from me, for I am gentle and humble in heart, and you will find rest for your souls" (Matthew 11:28-29). Rest for our souls. Isn't that what we all want?

Like this woman, we may have "a spirit of infirmity" (Luke 13:11 NKJV), a sickness of the soul. That is an interesting way to explain her illness. More than just a crippled back, her spirit was crippled as well.

Linda Hollies, in her book *Jesus and Those Bodacious Women*, brings this point home:

> There are many spirits that can cause you to walk around in a bent-over state. They might be your color, your gender, your age, your marital state, your family, or they could be abuse, injustice, resentment, oppression, despair, loneliness, your economic state, or even a physical challenge. It makes no difference what has hurt you in the past, it makes no

difference how old you were when the trauma affected your life, and it makes no difference what your wealth, position, or status is. For the evil one comes to steal, kill, and destroy and each one of us is a candidate for being bent and bowed.[6]

Bent and bowed. The weight of the world on our shoulders. Little by little. Day by day. Heaviness too difficult to bear. A spirit of infirmity. Crippled by shame, fear, pain, disappointment, depression, poverty, insecurity, inferiority, inadequacy, or broken dreams. Satan, the one who orchestrates the spirit of infirmity, wants to cripple us into inactivity so that our walk becomes a shuffle, our voice becomes a whisper, our vision becomes a blur.

Who put the chains on her in the first place? Jesus said Satan had her bound (Luke 13:16). In reality, all sickness was ushered into the world when Adam and Eve believed Satan's lie over God's truth and ate the forbidden fruit. For the 33 years that Jesus walked the earth, He was in a life-and-death struggle with evil. The battleground is the world, and humans are the pawns of the evil one. Note the language, "locked up" and "set free." This is about much more than physical healing. It is about spiritual freedom. And when Jesus said on the cross, "It is finished," it was. Now, because of Jesus' victory over the enemy through His death and resurrection, we are more than conquerors through faith in Him (Romans 8:37).

Don't miss this. Jesus said, "Woman, you are *set free* from your infirmity." There are those words again—*set free*. The words paint a picture of chains and manacles falling from a prisoner's shackled body. Another translation says it this way, "Woman, you are *released* from your infirmity!" (Luke 13:12 AMP). The irons of oppression that held her prisoner to this crippled frame gave way and fell at Jesus' feet as He unlocked the chains that had her bound.

Jesus came to set us free, and that freedom comes in many forms. Whatever Satan is using to bind you, Jesus came to free you. Free from...and free to. I can't say that enough. For far too long we've looked at freedom only in terms of what we are free from, but freedom encapsulates so much more than a shedding of chains. Jesus set us free to live the abundant life by being all He has created us to be and accomplishing all He has planned for us to do. Setting this infirm woman straight (literally) was only the beginning for her. She was now at the front of the synagogue, in a place where women were kept at bay. Now what? Do you think she grabbed hold of her healing and then ran back to the women's quarters where she belonged?

We don't know for sure, but I think she just sat right down in front of Jesus, just like Mary of Bethany, and continued listening to Jesus teach. That is, after she danced around praising God until she was breathless. There is much we don't know, but this is what we do know. Jesus did not send her back to the women's portico.

Freed to Walk in Confidence

When my brother was a teenager, my mother used to threaten him when he hunched over at the dinner table. "If you don't sit up," she would say, "I'm going to buy you a back brace from Sears." I don't even know if Sears made back braces back then, but it sounded like a pretty good threat to me.

Then I had a son who seemingly grew to six feet overnight. He didn't know what to do with all that height, so he slumped. I tried my best not to say, "If you don't sit up, I'm going to buy you a back brace from Sears."

Then one night my father-in-law took care of it for me. We were measuring and marking various family members' heights on the dining room door frame. (Yes, you read that correctly—the dining room. Some battles are just not worth fighting.) My 77-year-old father-in-law, who was about 5'10", stood with his back against the doorframe. Then he took a deep breath and extended his curved back to its fullest upright position. We marked him at 6'3".

I watched Steven's eyes grow wider as Papa grew taller. He saw firsthand the difference it made to stand up straight. Papa was huge, but his bent-over frame hid his once stately stature. Steven caught a glimpse of the strappingly strong frame that we had known. From that day on, my son stood straight and tall. Never once since then have I seen him slump.

That's what I'm hoping for you. That's why I wrote this book. My hope is that you will see women who have stood to their full stature and want to do the same. No more slumping in self-doubt or hunching in halfhearted conviction, but instead standing up to the full stature of a confident woman who knows she is equipped by God, empowered by the Holy Spirit, and enveloped in Jesus Christ.

There are many emotions that cause us to slump spiritually and become crippled emotionally. Worry wears us down. Regret ruins our confidence. Hatred hardens our hearts. Unforgiveness uglies our souls. Bitterness binds our hearts. Insecurity incapacitates our capabilities.

I was crippled for many years. I listened to words from my past telling me I was "ugly," "not good enough," and "worthless." Inferiority, insecurity, and inadequacy were my three closest companions. I didn't like these three lurking shadows, but they followed me everywhere I went. Stalkers, that's what they were. They stalked me, yelling taunts and accusations that no one heard but me.

The more I listened to them, the more emotionally crippled I became. Then one day Jesus called me up front. I didn't want to go, mind you. I had grown comfortable hiding in the back where I felt I belonged. I could hear just fine from my seat along the wall. The lighting wasn't as good, but it was enough to get by.

But then Jesus saw me and called me forward. It wasn't that He hadn't seen me all along. After all, He is El Roi, the God Who Sees. There was never a day when I had not been in His sight. But now the time had come for Him to set me straight in every way. So He called me up front where others could see what He was about to do. Jesus placed His nail-scarred hand under my chin and lifted my eyes to meet His. "Sharon, you are free from your infirmity of self-doubt."

Not long after that, words began to flow. From pen to paper, God filled me with words that overflowed to encourage and equip other sisters who needed to experience the same liberating freedom in Christ.

You know what, I'm sure some onlookers gasped at my courage and glared at my audacity as I stepped out of the shadows onto center stage. *Who does she think she is?* they might have thought.

And I can answer that question. I am a crippled woman whom Jesus set free. He calls me a child of God, light of the world, salt of the earth, bride of Christ, redeemed, holy, chosen, ambassador, saint, bride…and that's just for starters. And, friend, if you know Jesus Christ as Savior, then that's exactly what He calls you too!

So here I am today and you are holding one of my books in your hand. A previously emotional cripple set straight and shored up by God.

Is there something in your life that is crippling your spirit? Unforgiveness? Bitterness? Resentment? Guilt? Sorrow? Worry? Regret? Comparison? If so, cut it loose, cast it off, throw it away. God calls us sheep, and sheep are not pack animals. We are not meant to carry such burdens with these scrawny legs of ours. If we try, we will only bend under pressure we were never meant to bear.

Oh, friend, He is calling you right now. Whatever has been holding you back from being all that God has called you to be and do all that God has fashioned you to do…Jesus has come to set you free! Stand up straight! Do you feel the press of His hand on the crook of your back? Do you feel His index finger under the point of your chin?

There's no doubt in my mind that you are holding this book because Jesus is calling you from the shadows to join Him center stage. He sees you and now is the time. You've been sitting in the back, in your crippled state far too long. It is time. "Woman, you are set free from your infirmity."

Set me free from my prison,
that I might praise your name.

PSALM 142:7

11

The Syrophoenician Persistent Parent

Freed from Feelings of Inferiority
Freed to Grasp Her True Worth

Belva held her twitching daughter in her arms. With eyes rolled back and thrashing limbs, the child convulsed and stiffened her limbs uncontrollably.

"Oh, Mara," the distraught mother cried. "When will this ever end?"

For years little Mara had violently convulsed in predictable synchronized intervals. The child often cried out in loud screeching voices, threw herself against the walls of their one-room home, and cut her arms with rocks and broken pottery until her blood flowed.

Belva and her daughter lived in Tyre, a Gentile Phoenician city that bordered Galilee along the Mediterranean Sea. She was from Canaanite descent—a people who had been enemies of the Jews since they marched into the Promised Land hundreds of years before. The Jews despised the entire region from Tyre to Sidon and avoided it at all costs.

But among the ungodliness that permeated the city, word of Jesus' miracles and teaching drifted along the streets. Belva drank in the stories like rain on the parched, cracked streets upon which she walked. How she longed for a drop of hope to fall on her weary soul. One story caught her attention more than any other.

"Belva, have you heard?" a neighbor began. "Jesus delivered a boy much like your Mara."

"Tell me," Belva asked hungrily. "What happened?"

"A boy in Galilee had an evil spirit that seized him and caused him to scream out for no reason at all. The spirit threw him into convulsions and he foamed at the mouth. It was destroying the boy, and his father, for that matter."

"Oh, that poor family. What did Jesus do?"

"Well, He was just returning from a trip with three of His disciples. I believe their names were Peter, James, and John. His other disciples had remained back in the village while they were away. This father took his son to them for healing. But nothing happened. They couldn't do a thing.

"But then Jesus and His three friends walked into the crowd, and this father fell at his feet.

"'Teacher, I beg You to look at my son, for he is my only child. A spirit seizes him and he suddenly screams. It throws him into convulsions so that he foams at the mouth. It scarcely ever leaves him and is destroying him.'"

"That sounds just like my Mara," Belva cried, her heart quickening.

"While the father was pleading with the Teacher, the boy fell to the ground in a convulsion."

"Oh, my!" Belva cried with her hand over her mouth.

"Then Jesus rebuked the evil spirit. 'Come out of him!' He cried. And, just like that, the demon was gone. Jesus picked up the boy and handed him back to his father."

Tears filled Belva's eyes as she listened to this miraculous account. *If only I could go to Jesus. But He wouldn't have anything to do with the likes of me, a woman. Especially a despised Gentile woman with Canaanite heritage. That was the story of a man and his son. Does God even care about a woman and her little girl?*

"Some say He is the Messiah—the Son of David. Who knows? Too bad Jesus won't be coming here," her friend continued. "He would never step foot in this forsaken place."

And with a shrug, Belva's friend walked away.

"Oh, God," Belva prayed, "is there any way You could make an exception for one so lowly as me? I know I am from a cursed race, a despised people, but my daughter is being destroyed. She is only a child. I am not asking for me. I am begging for her. Please send Jesus my way. Please heal my little daughter. You are our only hope." And with those final words on her lips, Belva cried herself to sleep.

"He's here! He's here!" A raucous crowd outside Belva's window startled her from her slumber. She rubbed the sleep from her eyes and roused herself out of bed. Quickly she ran to the window and peeked to see what the commotion was all about. Then she saw Him. No one had to tell her the identity of the stranger walking past her home. Somehow she just knew.

"It's Jesus!" she cried.

Belva grabbed her shawl and dashed from her home. Hope was passing by, and she fell at His feet to block the way. "Lord, Son of David, have mercy on me! My little girl suffers from demon-possession."

Jesus didn't answer the woman but kept walking along the dusty road.

Again she cried, "Lord, Son of David, please have mercy on me! My daughter is…she is suffering terribly."

"Send this woman away," the disciples urged. "She keeps crying out after us. Get rid of her."

Jesus then paused and spoke to the woman. "I wasn't sent to you, but to the lost sheep of Israel."

Kneeling humbly at His feet, she sobbed. "Lord, help me!"

"It is not right to take bread meant for children and toss it to the dogs," Jesus replied.

"Yes, Lord," she gently whispered, "but even the dogs eat the crumbs that fall from their master's table."

Jesus held out His hand and pulled this woman to her feet—this woman to whom He had been sent. "Woman, you have great faith! Your request is granted."

Belva ran home to find her daughter lying on her bed, brushing her doll's hair, and in her right mind. She never had another seizure.

Years later, as she often did, Mara asked her mother to tell her a story as she tucked her into bed. "Mommy, tell me the story of Jesus again."

A Closer Look

I love this story on so many levels. I've had to stop and dry my eyes several times before proceeding. Here was a woman that the religious world would have steered clear of, and yet God steered Jesus right to her front door.

Let's walk through the details and discover just how much God loves and esteems women—even those...especially those...who society thought weren't worth the ground they walked on.

Jesus withdrew to the region of Tyre and Sidon (Matthew 15:21).

After Jesus' earthly ministry had begun with turning the water into wine, He had performed miracles left and right. Just a few days before this encounter with the Syrophoenician woman, He had fed five thousand men plus women and children with five loaves and two fish. Later that evening, as the disciples struggled to stay afloat in a life-threatening storm on the sea of Galilee, Jesus defied nature and walked on the water to calm their sinking hearts and the turbulent sea. Even as they sailed away to the distant shore, Jesus knew the religious leaders were behind closed doors plotting His death.

He needed to get away from the hustle and bustle to catch His breath...at least that is how it appeared to the disciples. But rather then going to a retreat center for a respite, or even to Mary and Martha's for a good meal, Jesus headed to the city of Tyre, some 30 miles away. For several days they traveled on foot over rough and rocky terrain.

Matthew used the word "withdrew." Jesus "withdrew to the region of Tyre and Sidon" (Matthew 15:21). He didn't just leave, He withdrew to be by Himself—to get away from the crowds.

I am sure the disciples questioned their new itinerary. *If Samaria wasn't bad enough, now we're going to Tyre! That heathen land of the cursed Canaanites! What is He thinking?*

Tyre was a trade capital whose position on the coast provided easy access to foreign trade. But along with the bountiful commerce emerged bountiful idol worship. Tyre and Sidon became centers for the worship of Baal and Asherah, where prostitution and human sacrifice were the norm.

Why would Jesus want to go there? they must have wondered.

Jesus had already said that it was the sick who need a doctor (Matthew 9:12). And this is exactly the sort of place where a doctor would head.

Mark tells us, "Jesus left that place and went to the vicinity of Tyre. He entered a house and did not want anyone to know it" (Mark 7:24). But you just can't keep news like that quiet. Jesus was in town!

> *A Canaanite woman from that vicinity came to him, crying out, "Lord, Son of David, have mercy on me! My daughter is suffering from terrible demon-possession" (Matthew 15:22).*

Matthew calls her a Canaanite. Apparently he couldn't forget that this gal was from a race of people that were longtime enemies of the Jews. Mark simply refers to her as a Greek, born in Syrian Phoenicia (Mark 7:26). Either way, she was a Gentile.

Did you notice that not an ounce of pride was in this woman's plea? She didn't care what anyone thought. She was begging for the life of her child. By her greeting, we get a hint that she believed Jesus was the Messiah. "Son of David" was a term that was associated with the coming Messiah, and she addressed Jesus as such.

Do you think approaching a man in public was risky for her? Do you think she was stepping out on a limb? Listen, she was so far out on a limb you can almost hear the branch cracking beneath her . feet. But she didn't care. There wasn't anything she wouldn't do for her daughter. She was a gutsy risk-taker, and making a public fool of herself was immaterial.

> *Jesus did not answer a word. So his disciples came to him and urged him, "Send her away, for she keeps crying out after us" (Matthew 15:23).*

Does it bother you that Jesus didn't answer her right away? Does His silence cause your heart to wince? I'll admit that when I read the scenario, I find myself holding my breath at Jesus' initial reaction. This must have screamed rejection to this wounded woman, but Jesus had something up His sleeve. He was using this as a teaching moment in the lives of the disciples and in the lives of all who would read their words for years to come.

Oh, dear friend, just because we don't hear an immediate response from God does not mean He is not listening. It does not mean that He has rejected our request. It may simply mean that He just has something else in mind or wants to take us to a deeper place of understanding. He may be taking us to a place that is so good, our minds need the pause to find it. What we do see and hear of God's working is miniscule compared to the magnificent workings we cannot see.

The disciples hadn't quite grasped Jesus' compassion for the human race. "Be quiet," they scolded the blind man who begged for sight. "Get those kids out of here," they scolded the parents who brought their children to Jesus for a blessing." "Send her away," they encouraged Jesus when this persistent mother kept pleading for the life of her child. But she persisted...and God hears the prayers of the persistent.

In Luke's Gospel, Jesus told His disciples a parable to show them that they should always pray and not give up. He said,

> In a certain town there was a judge who neither feared God nor cared about men. And there was a widow in that town who kept coming to him with the plea, "Grant me justice against my adversary." For some time he refused. But finally he said to himself, "Even though I don't fear God or care about men, yet because this widow keeps bothering me, I will see that she gets justice, so that she won't eventually wear me out with her coming!" (Luke 18:2-5).

In the Gospel of Matthew, He said,

> Keep on asking and it will be given you; keep on seeking
> and you will find; keep on knocking [reverently] and [the
> door] will be opened to you. For every one who keeps on
> asking receives; and he who keeps on seeking finds; and
> to him who keeps on knocking, [the door] will be opened
> (Matthew 7:7-8 AMP).

Jesus had taught His disciples the principles of persistence in
prayer. Now He was taking them on a field trip to see a living
example of the spiritual truth. He was going to answer her—after
all, that's why He came to town. But not yet...

> *He answered, "I was sent only to the lost sheep of Israel."*
> *(Matthew 15:24).*

Well, that is not the answer I was thinking of. Perhaps Jesus was
fishing to bring her bold faith to the surface. So He set the bait and
waited a moment more.

> *The woman came and knelt before him. "Lord, help me!" she*
> *said (Matthew 15:25).*

She had no more words. She didn't know what else to say. "Lord,
help me!" Have you ever said those same words? On the days when
the waves of emotions swell over us, the undertow of sorrow pulls beneath us, or the fog of confusion settles around us, "Lord, help me!"

I have cried and prayed until there are no more words. God is
not impressed with long, flowery prayers. He is impressed, however,
with a prayer of faith offered in humility.

> *He replied, "It is not right to take the children's bread and*
> *toss it to their dogs" (Matthew 15:26).*

At first glance His words sound demeaning, but in the context
of Jesus' life and actions, we know that was never His intent. So we
must dig deeper. What was He doing? Why did He respond with
such a rebuff? I believe Jesus was teaching—always teaching. He

knew her heart before He even saw her face. He wanted the disciples to know it as well.

Matthew had already recorded stories of Jesus healing a Gentile centurion's servant and delivering a demon-possessed man in the Gentile region of Gadarenes (Matthew 8:5-13,28-34). Her being a Gentile was not a problem to Jesus. This lets us know that Jesus had a specific motive for His response to the woman. He was fishing for faith.

Gentiles were often referred to as dogs, referring to the disease-ridden scrawny scavengers that roamed the streets, but the word Jesus used here is actually more like puppies or domesticated pets. Still, it was not a term of endearment. The woman understood Jesus' implications, but she didn't let it deter her mission. She wasn't offended but acknowledged her lowly estate.

> "Yes, Lord," she said, "but even the dogs eat the crumbs that
> fall from their masters' table" (Matthew 15:27).

Once again, He used the faith of a woman to teach the disciples faith's power. As if to say, "Watch this, boys, " Jesus prods her to expose the faith hidden deep within. His divine purpose was the surfacing of a faith that bubbled just below the surface.

With a quick wit and humble response, her faith was exposed. I believe Jesus smiled at her words.

> Then Jesus answered, "Woman, you have great faith! Your
> request is granted." And her daughter was healed from that
> very hour (Matthew 15:28).

I love how Eugene Peterson paraphrases Jesus' comments to our Syrophoenician sister: "'Oh, woman, your faith is something else. What you want is what you get!' Right then her daughter became well" (MSG).

Only two people in the Gospel of Matthew are commended for their great faith: the centurion who asked Jesus to heal his servant recorded in Matthew 8:10 and this Canaanite woman in Tyre. Both came to Jesus on behalf of someone they loved dearly. Both were Gentiles who believed in the Jewish Messiah who came for all.

Freed from Feelings of Inferiority

Do you think this woman caught Jesus off guard? That she surprised Him with her persistence? Not on your life. Just as Jesus "had to go to Samaria," I believe He had to go to Tyre. You see, this woman was there. A woman who had cried out to God for the life of her child. And on God's kingdom calendar, written on Jesus' celestial Day-Timer, her name appeared.

We don't know her name. I've simply put a name with the face so we can picture her in our mind's eye. But here's the thing. Jesus knew her name. Jesus knew her address. Jesus knew her need. And sister, He knows your name, your address, and your need as well. No matter what you may think of yourself, Jesus thinks you are worth the trip!

The Syrophoenician woman could not go to Jesus, but He could certainly go to her. And He did. Neither Matthew nor Mark tells us of any other activity that occurred in Tyre. As far as we know, Jesus didn't come in contact with any other residents or perform any other miracles. Would Jesus go through all that trouble for one woman and her little girl? You bet He would! That's how significant God's daughters are to Him.

After this encounter, "Jesus left there and went along the Sea of Galilee" (Matthew 15:29). His assignment was complete.

Sometimes He sends one of His very own to minister to us. The encounter may be so unexpected and so convoluted that we know there is no other way it could have happened except by divine appointment.

Heather experienced that in her own life. She and her family lived in North Dakota, hundreds of miles from their hometown. After her grandmother died and her mother-in-law was hospitalized for triple bypass surgery, she longed to move closer to her extended family in Arkansas. After applying for a transfer, her husband, Bob, was chosen for a job in Little Rock. They packed up their three boys, Robert, Cameron, and Caleb, and headed south.

During a routine eye exam of their oldest son, Robert, the optometrist discovered a bulging optic nerve. He was then referred to an ophthalmologist at Saline Memorial Hospital for further evaluation. A CAT scan showed that 15-year-old Robert had a brain tumor. They were then instructed to take Robert to Arkansas Children's Hospital. Dr. Burson, one of the neurosurgeons, was there waiting for them.

An MRI showed that the tumor appeared to have tentacles wrapped around the brain stem and needed to be removed right away. If the tentacles were intertwined around the brain stem, and if the stem was damaged during the resection and removal of the tumor, there was a chance that Robert would not be able to walk or talk after surgery. The doctor assured the weary parents that he would do his best to remove the tumor without damaging the brain stem, but there was a risk.

Friends and family rallied around this little family with prayer and support. A man who worked with Heather at FamilyLife Today was a great source of encouragement. "Sandy had been diagnosed with a brain tumor years earlier," Heather explained. "He came to encourage Robert that night in the hospital. It was so encouraging to see a man who had undergone brain surgery walking and talking normally. The Lord used him and his story to fill our hearts with great hope."

Then another burst of hope came through an e-mail. The son of a woman who worked with Heather also had a brain tumor removed by the same neurosurgeon that would be removing Robert's. "Dr. Burson studied under one of the greatest neurosurgeons in the country," she began. "And he is a follower of Jesus Christ too."

The next morning Robert was taken into surgery. Hours later, the smiling doctor reported that the tumor had been safely removed and the tentacles had not yet wrapped around the brain stem as the MRI had suggested.

God had orchestrated the Molden family's move from North

Dakota to Arkansas at just the right time. He knew where the tumor was hiding. He knew where one of the best neurosurgeons in the country was practicing. This was no coincidence but a God-incident. Initially, they moved across the country to be closer to extended family. But the reality is that God moved them there to take care of one of their greatest treasures…Robert, their son.

Would God do that for just one family in Little Rock, Arkansas? Absolutely. There are no insignificant children in God's family. As someone once said, "If God had a wallet, your picture would be in it." Each and every one of us has great significance to the Father who cares for us as if we were His only child. If you have ever felt insignificant in your little part of the world, know that nothing could be further from the truth. God treasures you, my friend. You are important to Him.

Freed to Grasp Her True Worth

We know Jesus walked into a time in history when women were considered insignificant, inferior, and incompetent. Men treated them with indifference, indignation, and inequality. But Jesus cut across cultural and religious barriers to show honor and respect to God's female image bearers. At first glance, Jesus' comments to the Syrophoenician woman seem demeaning at best. But upon closer inspection, we discover His magnificent means of bringing her faith to fruition.

In the book of Genesis, we meet another woman who felt insidiously insignificant. Her name was Hagar, the maidservant of Abraham's wife, Sarah. After years of infertility, Sarah convinced her husband to sleep with her maid—a common custom during those days. Hagar became pregnant. Sarah became jealous. The spiteful wife mistreated her maid until she could take it no more. Hagar ran away to the desert. Mistreated and misused. Alone and afraid. Insignificant and inferior. Disregarded and disposed. Ever felt that way yourself?

But God stepped in at her greatest point of need. God looked down on this broken woman and sent an angel to give her comfort and direction. "Go back to your mistress and submit to her…I will increase your descendants so that they are too numerous to count."

Hagar was surprised that God would consider her—a lowly servant girl. She was moved by God's grace, and she gave Him the name, "El Roi," the God Who Sees. "You are the God who sees me" (Genesis 16).

It is so easy to fall into the trap of feeling insignificant and inferior. *Nobody loves me. Nobody cares about me. I don't matter. God is too busy for me. God doesn't care about my pain.* But, sister, those are lies… all lies. God loves you so much He sent His Son to die for you— and the ground is level at the foot of the cross. You matter so much to God that He knows every hair on your pretty little head. God never sleeps but hears your every prayer. Jesus understands your pain because He has experienced it Himself.

In the story of Jesus and the Syrophoenician mother, we see Jesus once again going out of His way to minister to a desperate, seemingly insignificant woman. This trend certainly was cause for pause among the disciples. It certainly wasn't what they expected. Jesus consistently elevated women to heights of significance and dignity that ran contrary to all they had ever known. Jesus loves shattering race, rank, and religious barriers to call women center stage. He did it then. He does it now.

God freed this Syrophoenician woman from feelings of inferiority by sending His Son on a special assignment just for her. Why? Because she was worth it. And so are you.

> *There is neither Jew nor Greek, slave nor free, male*
> *nor female, for you are all one in Christ Jesus.*
>
> GALATIANS 3:28

12

THE GRACIOUS GIVER

Freed from Worry About Tomorrow
Freed to Trust God for Today

Beatrice woke as the morning sun peeked through the closed shutters of her sparse bedroom. Every joint in her tired old body creaked like a grinding wheel in dire need of good oiling. Her arthritic hands rubbed sleepy eyes, and then she instinctively reached to the empty space where her husband slept so many years ago.

"Another Sabbath to worship Jehovah," she murmured, smiling. "Lord, thank You for the health and strength to travel to Your house today. Thank You for all the many blessings You have showered on this old woman."

Beatrice slipped on her worn woolen garment, wound her gray-streaked hair around her head, and splashed yesterday's water on her wrinkled face. Slipping her hand into her money pouch hidden behind a grouping of jars, she fumbled her fingers to gather an offering for the temple coffers.

A heavy sigh escaped her lips as her hand retrieved two small coins. She put her hand back in the pouch and ran her fingers from side to side. This time she came up empty.

Looking at the two small coins in her hand, she continued her conversation with God. "I wish I had more to give You today, but,

Lord, this is all I have." Not once did Beatrice wonder how she would buy wheat for her next meal. She knew God would provide. He always did.

Beatrice shuffled out the door and through the busy streets of Jerusalem. The population was more than doubled because of the Passover celebration. Jews from miles around gathered at the temple during the holy week.

People, people, everywhere people, Beatrice thought to herself. *And not one notices an old worthless widow like me.*

She kept her eyes down as she climbed the first set of steps to the women's court in the temple. *I'm glad I'm not a man or priest. I don't think I could climb all those stairs to get to the upper levels.*

The widow made her way to the same offering receptacle she always used. When she raised her eyes to place the two small coins in the container, she noticed a man sitting right beside it. It was Jesus! Color rose to her cheeks as she realized that the Teacher was watching her. Beatrice cringed with embarrassment as she dropped her two small coins into the large box. *What must He think of me? Only two copper coins.*

When she looked up again and met Jesus' gaze, He grinned from ear to ear and nodded His approval. Every wrinkle in her face crinkled as she returned the smile. But what He said next almost made her feel like a spry young girl again.

"Peter, John, James. Friends, come over here," Jesus called. "You're looking around at all these people dropping their coins in the temple treasury, and I'm sure you have noticed that some of the wealthy made large donations. At least, they are hoping you've noticed. But I tell you the truth, this poor widow has put more in the treasury than all the others. They all gave out of their wealth. That was no sacrifice at all. It was just surplus. But this woman gave out of her poverty." Jesus placed His hand on Beatrice's shoulder. "She gave all she had to live on. Her gift is more precious to God than all the others combined."

Beatrice gently bowed and turned to leave. Jesus laughed to Himself, thinking about what she would find in her money pouch the next day. Oh, how God loved blessing His children.

A Closer Look

This is the last recorded incident in Jesus' public ministry before He makes final preparations for the cross. All the way from Galilee to Jerusalem, He had been teaching the disciples about the high cost of discipleship. "He who humbles himself will be exalted" (Luke 14:11). "Anyone who does not carry his cross and follow me cannot be my disciple" (Luke 14:27). "In the same way, any of you who does not give up everything he has cannot be my disciple" (Luke 14:33). Now, as they arrived at the temple in Jerusalem, Jesus shows them a living example of His spiritual teaching.

This was Passover week, and Jerusalem was teeming with Jews participating in the festivities. Jesus had been teaching for the better part of the day, knowing that this would be the last chance He had to speak to the multitudes in the temple. After teaching, He moved to where the offerings were placed to teach His disciples about true giving.

Remember, during the time of Jesus, the temple was partitioned off in various segments allowing only certain types of people in each area. Each partition was separated by a set of steps that led up to the next one. Higher and higher the Jewish leaders elevated themselves from the rest of the common folks.

I want you to keep that picture in mind. Let's walk up the steps from the court of Gentiles and join Jesus in the court of women.

> *Jesus sat down opposite the place where the offerings were put and watched the crowd putting their money into the temple treasury (Mark 12:41).*

The court of women held the temple treasury and is where all worshippers gave their tithes and offerings. Thirteen boxes, shaped like inverted megaphones or trumpets, lined the walls to receive the money. In this particular story, it was Passover week, so there was a steady flow of pilgrims depositing their contributions.

Jesus, the Creator of the universe, the God-made-man, the Great High Priest, didn't go past gate 2, gate 3, gate 4, or gate 5. Rather, He stayed in the women's court with the common folk—with His people. But there was one woman in particular He was waiting for. He knew she was coming. He was expecting her.

> *Many rich people threw in large amounts. But a poor widow came and put in two very small copper coins, worth only a fraction of a penny (Mark 12:41-42).*

Picture Jesus pulling up a chair by a certain offering box. Oh, let's just say it was offering box number 5. Of course we don't know which one of the 13 offering boxes Jesus was watching, but the point is, He knew exactly which one she would be coming to. He was waiting for her…she just didn't know it.

One by one, wealthy attendees tossed their coins into the coffers. I can almost hear the clanging now. The more noise the offering made, the better. "Look at me! Look at me!" the loud clanging coins announced. "I'm giving a lot today. Why? Because I am important. I am wealthy. I am holy. Don't you wish you could be more like me?"

But then, here she comes. A shabbily dressed, worn old woman. Head hung low, unproud. She timidly approaches the offering box and gingerly places her treasure among the coins. The others "toss." She "places." Two small copper coins—the smallest coins in circulation in Palestine—just a fraction of a penny. Two of these lepton, as they were called, were worth $\frac{1}{64}$ of a denarius, a typical day's wage. But these coins were, in reality, worth more than any day's wages. They were all she had…and Jesus knew it.

Do you ever feel that other people don't really care about what is going on in your life? Do you feel insignificant in the grand scheme of things? I am sure this widow must have felt the same. *I'm nothing. I have nothing. I am invisible to these men with flowing robes and tasseled garb.*

Ever been there? I have. But she wasn't insignificant. Jesus was waiting for her arrival—for her gift. "For the eyes of the LORD range throughout the earth to strengthen those whose hearts are fully committed to him" (2 Chronicles 16:9).

> *Calling his disciples to him, Jesus said, "I tell you the truth, this poor widow has put more into the treasury than all the others. They all gave out of their wealth; but she, out of her poverty, put in everything—all she had to live on" (Mark 12:43-44).*

Jesus was waiting for this widow. He knew she was coming. And He used a seemingly insignificant woman to teach His disciples about significant giving.

The widow had two copper coins. I wonder what I would have done in the same situation. I think I would have been tempted to just give one to the temple treasury and keep one for myself. One for You. One for me. After all, God wouldn't want me to go hungry, would He?

I was speaking at a women's retreat in Canada, and several precious women from a group home were attending. It was apparent by their worn clothing that they didn't have many earthly possessions. One woman in particular, Becky, sat in a wheelchair with her clothes for the weekend in a brown paper bag. Her friend Clara simply held her belongings for the weekend in her lap.

I felt God nudge my heart. *Give them your two suitcases.*

I had packed two suitcases full of books for the weekend, and my clothes were in a simple carry on. God was telling me to leave those two suitcases behind for His lambs. I readily agreed.

That was on Friday night, but as the time drew near for me to leave, my conviction began to wane. *I really like those suitcases,* I whined. *Maybe I didn't hear Him right.*

On Saturday, before the last session, I saw Becky sitting near the front in her wheelchair, but Clara was nowhere in sight.

"Where's Clara," I asked the coordinator.

"She got sick and had to go home early."

In my mind I began thinking, *Okay, I'm just going to leave one suit-case behind. After all, Clara's not here, so maybe one will be enough.*

I was standing at the back of the room while the MC intro-duced me for our final session. "We are here to let go of our burdens today," she began. "We're going home in just a little while and we are not going to take any baggage with us. None of it! We are going to leave it all right here at the foot of the cross."

God had my attention. Leave your baggage. *Don't you even think about leaving* only one *of those suitcases and taking the other one home,* He seemed to say. *Don't leave anything behind.*

Well, I'm slow, but not altogether dense. Sometimes He gives us a second chance at obedience, as He did for me that day. But some-times He says it once and expects us to obey. When we don't, we miss the blessing.

The widow did not give one coin and keep one for herself. She gave all she had, fully trusting that God would take care of her every need. Commentators have pointed out that when Jesus said, "She out of her poverty put in all the livelihood that she had" (Luke 21:4), He used the word *bios* which means she gave her *life* itself.

Let me share one other nugget of gold from Jesus' response to our sister. When my family and I traveled to Yellowstone Park and Jackson Hole, Wyoming, several years ago, one of our goals was to see as many unusual animals as possible. For us that was anything other than a dog, cat, or bird. During the entire trip, we were on the lookout for moose, elk, buffalo, and other furry beasts with antlers. After several days we fell into the rhythm of looking for groupings of cars stopped alongside the road or crowds clustered in the woods. This signaled a sighting! As if holding up a neon sign, the assembly let us know we needed to stop. There was some magnificent crea-ture we needed to see.

Imagine with me for a moment. Jesus calls the disciples over to see the widow and her gift. Thirteen men gather round the offering box as Jesus shines His spotlight on her sacrificial act. Now, what else do you see? I see other people migrating to the scene. "What's so important?" "What's going on?" "What are you men looking at?" Then Jesus lifts His hand and directs their attention to one of God's magnificent creations. She simply nods and walks away. That, my friend, is truly a Kodak moment.

Freed from Worry About Tomorrow

What strikes me about this little woman is that she wasn't worried about tomorrow. She gave all she had and walked away confident that God would meet her every need.

There is another woman in the Old Testament who was faced with a similar dilemma. We don't know her name, but we do know that she was a Gentile living in a small town called Zarephath.

Elijah was a prophet living during those days, and often spoke out against King Ahab. Ahab and his wife, Jezebel, encouraged Baal worship and set up wooden poles in honor of the goddess Asherah. Prostitution was a type of temple worship, and the land was filled with evil at every turn. Elijah was very vocal about God's disapproval of idol worship.

In response to the evil that filled the land, Elijah prophesied: "As the LORD, the God of Israel, lives, whom I serve, there will be neither dew nor rain in the next few years except at my word" (1 Kings 17:1).

You can imagine that this did not put Elijah on Ahab's short list of friends. As a matter of fact, he was on Ahab's most wanted list of enemies. So God sent Elijah to hide in the Kerith Ravine, east of the Jordan. There he drank from the brook to quench his thirst. Not only that, but God ordered ravens to bring Elijah bread and meat in the morning and in the evening. Talk about fast food!

Eventually, though, the brook dried up. Could God have prevented the brook from drying up? Absolutely! But He had yet another miracle in mind. A widow in Zarephath needed a blessing.

"Go at once to Zarephath of Sidon and stay there," God instructed. "I have commanded a widow in that place to supply you with food" (1 Kings 17:9). The only problem was, apparently God didn't tell the widow His plan.

When Elijah finally meets up with her, she didn't greet him with great enthusiasm. She was gathering sticks.

Elijah asked, "Would you bring me a little water in a jar so I may have a drink?" (verse 10).

As she was turning away to get it, he called out, "And bring me, please, a piece of bread" (verse 11).

Bread. Now that was a splendid idea...if she had any to give. But this woman, this widow, was in dire straights. "I don't have any bread," she replied. "I have only a handful of flour in a jar and a little oil in a jug. I am gathering a few sticks to take home and make a meal for myself and my son, that we may eat it—and die" (verse 12).

Now, that is a desperate woman if I've ever seen one. She was gathering sticks to build a fire to prepare her last meal. I can hear her now. "This is it, son. This is all I've got. I'm so sorry."

And then here comes this man of God wanting bread. I imagine she thought, *Oh sure, and would you like a lamb chop to go along with that?*

But, you see, God saw her. She was not alone. And as He often does, He asked her to give all that she had so that He could give her all she needed.

"Don't be afraid," Elijah said to her. "Go home and do as you have said. But first make a small cake of bread for me from what you have and bring it to me, and then make something for yourself and your son. For this is what the LORD, the God of Israel says: 'The jar of flour will not be used up and the jug of oil will not run dry until the day the LORD gives rain on the land'" (1 Kings 17:13-14).

What would I have done? Hmm. Kept maybe a handful for myself just in case? Given Elijah half a cake? Made two cakes and pretended that what I gave him WAS the whole cake?

What did she do? She did exactly what the woman did at the offering box. She gave God everything. I'm crying sitting here thinking about it. Let me say it again. She gave God everything. She did not hold anything back. This didn't affect only her. It affected her son as well.

Could she trust the life of her son to God? That is a different story. Sometimes it is easier for a mother to trust God for her own life than the lives of her children. But this widow from Zarepath did trust Him. She gave all she had.

Let's go back to Elijah's words: "Don't be afraid." Does that remind you of another greeting to one of our New Testament leading ladies? Gabriel spoke those same words to Mary. Those are the same words God speaks to all of us when we are about to take center stage and be used to build the kingdom. Obeying God always requires courage.

Then there is one little power packed sentence… "She went away and did as Elijah had told her" (verse 15). We can echo Elizabeth's words to Mary: "Blessed is she who has believed that what the Lord has said to her will be accomplished!" (Luke 1:45).

What happened next is amazing. "So there was food every day for Elijah and for the woman and her family. For the jar of flour was not used up and the jug of oil did not run dry, in keeping with the word of the LORD spoken by Elijah" (verses 15-16).

Oh, friend, power always follows obedience. God's power—God's providing power—followed this woman's obedience to give all she had.

So now, as we sit in the temple with Jesus, we see another widow—a widow approaching the offering coffer. What does she do? Like the widow in Zarephath, this widow gives all she has. I don't think for one minute Jesus let her walk away and live the rest of her life empty handed. I would love to know what happened to her as the days and weeks followed her sacrificial gift. Jesus gives us a hint in His other teachings.

"Give, and it will be given to you. A good measure, pressed down, shaken together and running over, will be poured into your lap. For with the measure you use, it will be measured to you" (Luke 6:38). In those days, men and women wore robes that were held together with belts. Extra fabric bloused out over the belt that served as a large pocket. Wearers used this large pocket to carry wheat. So when Jesus said that blessings would be poured into your lap, He was giving the picture of sustenance filling up and overflowing their pockets.

What is done in secret never goes unnoticed by God. "Your Father, who sees what is done in secret, will reward you" (Matthew 6:18). "Whoever sows generously will also reap generously" (2 Corinthians 9:6).

How precious that Jesus used the gift of an insignificant woman to teach the disciples about significant giving. She became an example to this burly bunch of men and to you and me.

Freed to Trust God for Today

Have you ever tried to out-give God? Go ahead, give it a try. But I can tell you, it just won't happen. You can't do it. We have so little to give and He has so much. John wrote, "How great is the love the Father has lavished on us, that we should be called children of God!" (1 John 3:1). Lavished! I just love that word.

Proverbs 31:10-31 tells of the virtuous woman who is worth more than rubies. In the listing of all her fine attributes, she is described as laughing "at the days to come" (verse 25). Why is she laughing? I think it is because she is not worried. She knows God will take care of her and her family. In no way am I implying that we sit around on our haunches and do nothing, just waiting for God to drop our daily bread in our laps. God is not too fond of laziness. Just one look at Miss Worth-More-Than-Rubies and you can see that she is a busy woman. At the same time, her last accolade reads, "A woman who fears the LORD is to be praised" (verse 30). It is a trust in the One who holds the future that serves as the solid foundation for her entire existence.

Jesus came to free us from worry about tomorrow by teaching us about God's provision for today. And when we give to God, He gives us so much more in return.

I love the story Alice Gray tells in her book *Stories for the Heart—The Second Collection*. It's about a little girl named Jenny. Alice tells it so well, I'm going to let her take the pen from here.*

---

* Alice Gray, *Stories for the Heart—The Second Collection*

The cheerful girl with bouncy golden curls was almost five. Waiting with her mother at the checkout stand, she saw them: a circle of glistening white pearls in a pink foil box.

"Oh please, Mommy. Can I have them? Please, Mommy, please!"

Quickly the mother checked the back of the little foil box and then looked back into the pleading blue eyes of her little girl's upturned face.

"A dollar ninety-five. That's almost $2. If you really want them, I'll think of some extra chores for you and in no time you can save enough money to buy them for yourself. You birthday's only a week away and you might get another crisp dollar bill from Grandma."

As soon as Jenny got home, she emptied her penny bank and counted out 17 pennies. After dinner, she did more than her share of chores and she went to the neighbor and asked Mrs. McJames if she could pick dandelions for ten cents. On her birthday, Granma did give her another new dollar bill and at last she had enough money to buy the necklace.

Jenny loved her pearls. They made her feel dressed up and grown up. She wore them everywhere—Sunday school, kindergarten, even to bed. The only time she took them off was when she went swimming or had a bubble bath. Mother said if they got wet, they might turn her neck green.

Jenny had a very loving daddy and every night when she was ready for bed, he would stop whatever he was doing and come upstairs to read her a story. One night when he finished the story, he asked Jenny, "Do you love me?"

"Oh, yes, Daddy. You know that I love you."

"Then give me your pearls."

"Oh, Daddy, not my pearls. But you can have Princess— the white horse from my collection. The one with the pink tail. Remember, Daddy? The one you gave me. She's my favorite."

"That's okay, Honey. Daddy loves you. Good night." And he brushed her cheek with a kiss.

About a week later, after the story time, Jenny's daddy asked again, "Do you love me?"

"Daddy, you know I love you."

"Then give me your pearls."

"Oh, Daddy, not my pearls. But you can have my baby doll. The brand-new one I got for my birthday. She is so beautiful and you can have the yellow blanket that matches her sleeper."

"That's okay. Sleep well. God bless you, little one. Daddy loves you." And as always, he brushed her cheek with a gentle kiss.

A few nights later when her daddy came in, Jenny was sitting on her bed with her legs crossed Indian-style. As he came close, he noticed her chin was trembling and one silent tear rolled down her cheek.

"What is it, Jenny? What's the matter?"

Jenny didn't say anything but lifted her little hand up to her daddy. And then she opened it, there was her little pearl necklace. With a little quiver, she finally said, "Here, Daddy. It's for you."

With tears gathering in his eyes, Jenny's kind daddy reached out with one hand to take the dime-store necklace, and with the other hand he reached into his pocket and pulled out a blue velvet case with a strand of genuine pearls and gave them to Jenny. He had had them all the time. He was just waiting for her to give up the dime-store stuff so he could give her genuine treasure.[1]

We can be sure that when we give God our meager offerings, He will bless us with the riches of heaven. Jesus showed us what He could do with a few loaves and fish. He doesn't need much to work with—and yet He requires it all.

Jesus said, "I have come that they might have life, and have it to the full" (John 10:10). The New American Standard Bible calls it abundant life. The Amplified Bible says, "I came that they may have and enjoy life, and have it in abundance (to the full, till it overflows)." *The Message* calls it "real and eternal life, more and better life than they ever dreamed of." That's what God wants for each of us.

But be sure of this—abundant life doesn't consist of mere earthly possessions. They *are* the dime-store stuff of life. Abundant living is a cornucopia of love, joy, and peace in knowing that God will provide for all our needs according to His riches in glory. He "is able to do immeasurably more than all we ask or imagine, according to his power that is at work within us" (Ephesians 3:20).

Jesus took His spotlight and shone it on one seemingly insignificant widow woman to show us a picture of significant sacrifice. While she might have felt worthless in the world's eyes, she was priceless to God.

The eyes of the LORD range throughout the earth to
strengthen those whose hearts are fully committed to him.

2 CHRONICLES 16:9

THE FINAL
CURTAIN CALL

13

GOD CALLING WOMEN CENTER STAGE

can still remember the day when God began dabbing His pen in His inkwell to write a new chapter in my life. For years I had been teaching Bible studies at my local church, volunteering as a peer counselor at a pregnancy care center, and helping my husband in his office. I had poured my heart and soul into being a mom to my son, Steven, and into being a wife to my husband, Steve. But God began stirring something in my heart. "I am doing a new thing!" God seemed to say. "Now it springs up; do you not perceive it?" (Isaiah 43:19).

It was a stirring. That's the best way I know to describe it. But I only knew the first line of the chapter. It would be a while before the words began filling the pages. After a year of seeking God and praying, God began to give me glimpses. He was moving me from local ministry into a much broader sphere of building His kingdom… and I wasn't sure I wanted to go.

I never thought of myself as "being in ministry." I just taught Bible studies and wrote them once in a while. But God was taking me in a new direction, and many questions began to swirl about in my mind. Many of the questions that Jan voiced in chapter 1 swirled in my head as well. How does God feel about women in ministry? I looked around and saw men playing leading roles, but where would

I fit in? Where *do* women fit in? What would God have women do to build His kingdom? What is ministry in the first place? How does God feel about women in general?

So I began a 15-year journey with God to answer those questions. Honestly, I thought this was just between God and me. I wasn't looking to answer these questions for anyone else. This was personal. But God had other plans, and you are now holding this book. Honestly, I was afraid to write it. The whole idea of women's roles, responsibilities, and relationships are a hornet's nest of strong opinions.

Through the years I've asked a lot of questions, read many respected theologians' interpretations and opinions, and examined more Greek and Hebrew words of Scripture than this Southern girl knew existed. But I just kept coming back to Jesus' ministry, miracles, and messages. Sometimes we humans can take a simple message and make it very complicated.

I know some will read the pages of this book and say, "Yes, but..." But...let's just walk the dusty streets with Jesus, listen to His words, watch His actions, and feel His heartbeat.

God spoke audibly to Jesus two times in the Gospels. "This is my Son, whom I love; with him I am well pleased," God said after Jesus' baptism (Matthew 3:17). Again, at the transfiguration, God said, "This is my Son, whom I love; with him I am well pleased." Then He added, "Listen to him!" (Matthew 17:5). So I have been trying to do just that...listen to Him.

Seeing the Father Through the Son

Let's go back to where we started in chapter 1. During one of Philip's last conversations with Jesus, he asked, "Lord, show us the Father and that will be enough for us" (John 14:8).

Seemingly frustrated, Jesus answered: "Don't you know me, Philip, even after I have been among you such a long time? Anyone who has seen me has seen the Father. How can you say, 'Show us the Father?' Don't you believe that I am in the Father, and that the Father is in me? The words I say to you are not just my own. Rather, it is the Father living in me, who is doing his work. Believe me when I say that I am in the Father and the Father is in me; or at least believe on the evidence of the miracles themselves" (John 14:9-11).

The writer of Hebrews tells us that Jesus is "the exact representation of [God's]being" (Hebrews 1:3). The original Greek word for "exact representation," *charakter*, describes the impress of a die or the impression of a coin. For example, if you took a coin and pressed it into wax, you would have an exact representation. So when we see Jesus, we see God.

On their way home from celebrating the Passover, Mary and Joseph noticed that their 12-year-old Son was missing from the caravan. After a three-day search, they found Jesus sitting among the teachers of the temple, listening and asking questions. When Mary questioned Him about why He stayed behind, Jesus responded, "I must be about my Father's business" (Luke 2:49 KJV). Twenty-one years later Jesus breathed His last with the words, "It is finished" (John 19:30). In the years sandwiched between these two statements, Jesus went about His Father's business of restoring broken mankind in every respect...including women.

So can we really know what God thinks about women? I believe we can. We have only to look at the words and actions of His Son. Time and time again God affirmed His love for His daughters through Jesus. All through the New Testament we see that Jesus was on a mission to restore fallen humanity in every sense of the word. Part of that redemptive process involved setting women free from the cultural oppression that had them bound and kept them from fulfilling God's original intent as His female image bearers. Jesus came to restore women and their rightful place of dignity as one half of a whole, as coheirs and coworkers with their male counterparts. His radical countercultural attitude toward women flew in the face of a patriarchal society that considered women less than men in all regards. He was a radical reformer who showed the world just what God thinks about women.

As we've seen, Jesus ignored cultural taboos and associated freely and openly with women. He spoke with women in broad daylight, even though the disciples disapproved. He welcomed the worshipful anointing of the woman with the sinful past, even though the religious leader thought it scandalous. He called the woman with the crippled back forward into the men's area of the temple, even though the synagogue ruler thought it inappropriate.

> Jesus' treatment of them [women] was always solicitous and supportive, as if he were assuming responsibility toward them for a long history of derogation and compensating for it with an outpouring of divine love. Predictably, Jesus saw the unnoticeable women—the little gray shadows who make themselves invisible so that they can blend into the background everywhere, the inconspicuous silent sufferers who can only think of themselves as negligible entities destined to exist on the fringes of life. Jesus saw them, identified their need, and in one gloriously wrenching moment, he thrust them to the center stage in the drama of redemption, with the spotlight of eternity beaming on them as he immortalized them into sacred history."[1]

Just as surely as Jesus overturned the money changers' tables in the temple, He overturned the exploitation and mistreatment of women (Matthew 21:12; Mark 11:15; John 2:15). He overruled the tightly held views of a society that kept women hidden in the fabric of life and blending inconspicuously into the background. Not only did He accept them as they were, He challenged them to become more. Even though He didn't give explicit instructions on the specific roles of men and women, He taught by example.

Jesus spoke with, mingled with, ministered to, and taught women just as easily as He did His male followers. He didn't limit His teaching illustrations to male-only experiences, but He clarified His principles with examples from women's lives as well. He compared God's joy over a lost soul coming to faith to the joy of a woman finding a lost coin (Luke 15:8-10). He taught of persistence in prayer by comparing it to a determined woman knocking on her neighbor's door (Luke 18:1-8). He compared heaven to yeast that a woman mixes into a large amount of flour until it works all through the dough (Matthew 13:33).

While spending time getting to know the leading ladies of the New Testament, we've seen how Jesus shone the spotlight on particular women to point out exemplary living, gracious giving, bold believing, winsome worship, fastidious faith—all character qualities Jesus highlighted through the women who crossed His path.

Jesus' attitude and actions toward women were in stark contrast to the religious leaders of His day. While the Pharisees avoided women, Jesus associated freely and spoke openly with them.

- He touched the unclean woman with the flow of blood.

- He taught the hungry female pupil in a room full of men.

- He encouraged Martha to join the classroom.

- He befriended the sisters of Bethany.

- He conversed with the thirsty Samaritan by the well.

- He revealed His true identity to the five-time divorcee.

- He welcomed the sinful woman's worship.

- He called the woman with the crippled back from the shadows.

- He invited Mary Magdalene to join His ministry team.

- He defended Mary of Bethany's gesture when anointing Him with perfume.

- He commended the Syrophoenician mother's faith.

- He applauded the widow's offering.

- He commissioned Mary Magdalene to go and tell the disciples of His resurrection.

He taught in places where women would be present: on a hillside, along the streets, in the marketplace, by a river, beside a well, and in the women's area of the temple. His longest recorded conversation in the New Testament was with a woman. And as we saw through the lives of several of the New Testament's leading ladies, some of His best students and most daring disciples were women.

And what was Jesus' first word after His resurrection? "Woman."

Jesus was willing to risk His reputation to save theirs. He was willing to go against the grain of religious leaders to liberate women from centuries of oppressive pious tradition. He delivered women from diseases and set them free from spiritual darkness. He took the fearful and forgotten and transformed them into the faithful and forever remembered. "I tell you the truth," He said, "wherever this gospel is preached throughout the world, what she has done will also be told, in memory of her" (Matthew 26:13).

Jesus saw women as image bearers of God whom He came to save and then to send. He freed them from their painful pasts and freed them to fulfill His purposeful plans. He made no distinction between male or female, married or single, old or young. He simply related to people in regard to their relationship to God or lack of one.

When it comes right down to it, it was the women who got it. The woman with the alabaster box understood that no matter what anyone thinks of us, Jesus deserves our worship. The woman at the well understood that no matter how broken our lives may be, Jesus is the long-awaited Messiah who makes all things new. Mary of Bethany understood that regardless of other people's expectations on our lives, spending time with Jesus is the most valuable choice we can make. Martha understood that regardless of the tragedy of present circumstances, Jesus is the Son of God who has power over life and death. These women understood Jesus' true identity when those closest to Him did not. The women were the ones who offered spiritual stamina with their presence and walked with Jesus until the very end, even at personal risk to themselves.

He emerged from the baptismal waters to wash away the boundary lines that kept women out of religious life in general. From Mary of Nazareth to Mary of Magdala, God used women to accomplish

His divine purposes. Brave women stepped forward. Courageous women spoke up. Committed women joined hands.

Embracing Freedom in the Savior

What Jesus did to lift up women has not been duplicated in any other world religion. Even today in Middle Eastern countries, women are often veiled in thick black chadors or burkas. Their faces are covered and they have no identity. Watch the news and notice the riots in the streets of the Middle East. Look at the streets during the busiest parts of the day. Women are conspicuously absent.

Many critics of Christianity suggest that women have been suppressed and oppressed in the church by encouraging male domination. And while that may be true in some cases, we cannot blame that on Jesus. He honored and respected women at every turn. He liberated them from the chains of an oppressive culture that kept them hidden away in the nooks and crannies of society and called them center stage to play leading roles in God's redemptive plan. He called them out of hiding and validated them as "daughters of Abraham." His actions echoed God's words at creation: "It is not good for the man to be alone" (Genesis 2:18).

Pastor Erwin Lutzer of Moody Bible Church, along with his wife, Rebecca, wrote:

> Jesus affirmed and validated women as equal partners in the family of God, which He came to establish. He proclaimed liberty to the captive. He did so, in part, by countering the debilitating cultural bias against women. Jesus clearly created a new family of brothers and sisters who shared the same heavenly Father (Mark 3:21-35). Thus, as members of the new family, women must have equality of spiritual privilege.[2]

I am captivated by words of freedom Jesus spoke to the women we have visited. "Woman, you are set free from your infirmity," Jesus told the crippled woman (Luke 13:12). "Daughter, your faith has healed you. Go in peace and be freed from your suffering," Jesus assured the woman with the chronic flow of blood (Mark 5:34). "Then neither do I condemn you. Go now and leave your life of sin," He said to the woman caught in adultery (John 8:11). All through the New Testament we see Jesus flinging prison doors open wide and brave women walking into freedom. Oh, that we would do the same. "It is for freedom that Christ has set us free" (Galatians 5:1).

Finding Significance Through Divine Purpose

Jesus is proof that God loves us. "A woman's high-calling as God's image bearer renders her incapable of insignificance, no matter what has gone wrong in her life or how much she has lost."[3] In our time together, we have met several women whose lives were impacted by Jesus. We've met a mother, two sisters, and a little girl. We've met single women, married women, and divorced women. We've met women who made mistakes and women who had been mistreated and abused by others. We've met women who had been beaten down by life with no hope at all…until Jesus.

While these women may have lived many years ago, they are really no different from you and me. Each one had hopes and dreams, fears and concerns, victories and defeats. And in each case, their dreams were laid shattered in a thousand tiny pieces before them…until Jesus.

I hope that you have seen a bit of yourself in each of these women. I pray that you have written your name into the script. For, you see, their story is your story, their suffering is your suffering, their hope is your hope, their victory is your victory…it is Jesus. He's the focus of each of their stories—the Hero who takes our breath away with His amazing love.

We saw Jesus pause in the middle of His busy day for the bleeding woman, stop His teaching to lift the chin of the bent and bowed, walk miles to deliver one small child, and wait patiently in the hot noon sun for the broken Samaritan to arrive. What kind of God does that? A God who loves His daughters. And how did the women respond to Jesus calling them center stage?

- Mary of Nazareth *stepped up* to accept her calling.
- Mary Magdalene *signed up* to join Jesus' ministry team.
- The woman with the chronic bleeding *spoke up* to tell of her miraculous healing.
- The woman caught in adultery *cleaned up* to start anew.
- The empty woman at the well *filled up* to evangelize an entire town.
- The woman with the alabaster jar *opened up* her heart to worship.
- Mary of Bethany *showed up* in the classroom.
- Martha *moved up* to the head of the class.
- The woman with the crippled back *walked up* to receive her healing.
- The Syrophoenician mother was *shored up* for bold believing.
- The widow *gave all up* as an example of sacrificial giving.

These leading ladies' stories show us that in God's family, girls are important too. They were strong women of faith who were bolstered by Jesus to come out of the shadows and take their place among the world changers of their day.

Where Do We Go from Here?

God always has important kingdom work for us to do. Paul tells us: "No eye has seen, no ear has heard, no mind has conceived what God has prepared for those who love him" (1 Corinthians 2:9). We were not meant to be mere stagehands or decorative props, but leading ladies working together alongside our brothers to impact the world for Christ.

Every little girl needs to grow up knowing she is valued, that she is made in the image of God. Every little girl needs to grow up expectantly waiting for her God-given potential to be released. These women gave us a taste—a glimpse.

Mary Magdalene is just one example. She did not lobby for a position of leadership. She did not argue for women's rights. She was content with the lowest place on Jesus' ministry team, doing whatever needed doing, giving financial support out of her own means, caring for Jesus' crucified body. But Jesus had a different calling for Mary Magdalene—one she certainly did not choose or aspire to. He called her center stage and gave her a leading role to announce the most important news in human history. She was an apostle to the apostles, commissioned by Jesus Himself.

After Jesus' ascension, both men and women waited in Jerusalem for the promised Holy Spirit. On the day of Pentecost, as the Holy Spirit descended with a gusty wind and tongues of fire, Peter stood and explained to curious onlookers what was taking place.

> This is what was spoken by the prophet Joel: "In the last days, God says, I will pour out my Sprit on all people. Your sons and daughters will prophesy, your young men will see visions, your old men will dream dreams. Even on my servants, both men and women, I will pour out my Spirit in those days, and they will prophesy" (Acts 2:16-18).

Peter explained to the people what Jesus had been showing them all along. God's grace, love, and power are extended to all people regardless of rank or race, gender or generation: sons and daughters, young and old, men and women. Paul would later pen: "There is neither Jew nor Greek, slave nor free, male nor female, for you are all one in Christ Jesus" (Galatians 3:28).

Where do we go from here? That is a question for you and God to decide. However, if God calls you center stage to accomplish His purpose for this generation, I pray that you will accept the role of a lifetime. And who knows? Perhaps you are holding this book in your hand and being challenged to fulfill God's purposes "for such a time as this."

A Note
FROM THE Author

If the message of *What God Really Thinks About Women* has stirred your heart to learn more about the plans God has for you, we can continue this journey together. The Bible reminds us, "Things which eye has not seen and ear has not heard, and which have not entered the heart of man, all that God has prepared for those who love Him (1 Corinthians 2:9 NASB).

Perhaps you've already felt God nudge you down a particular path and you simply need to take the next step of faith and say yes to Him. But if you are unsure where to go from here and would like to learn more about how to discern God's plans for your life, then we can continue learning and growing together. My follow-up book to *What God Really Thinks About Women* is *When Women Dare to Dream Again*, and it takes a closer look at how God fulfills and surpasses the dreams of every woman.

Can you risk the hope that God still has dreams for your life? That He hasn't forgotten you? Place your hand firmly in His, take a deep breath, and begin the exciting journey to a place you thought you'd never find: the dream God planned for you all along.

Look for *When Women Dare to Dream Again* coming soon.

Notes

Chapter 1—The World Jesus Stepped Into

1. Anne Dickason, "Anatomy and Destiny: The Role of Biology in Plato's Views of Women" as quoted in Carol C. Gould and Marx W. Wartofsky, eds., *Women and Philosophy: Toward a Theory of Liberation* (New York, NY: Putnam, 1976).

2. Bruce Marchiano, *Jesus, the Man Who Loved Women* (New York, NY: Howard Books, 2008), 51.

3. Carolyn Custis James, *When Life and Beliefs Collide* (Grand Rapids, MI: Zondervan Publishing House, 2001), 177.

4. C.S. Lewis, *Mere Christianity* (Westwood, NJ: Barbour and Company, Inc., 1952), 88.

5. Umberto Cassuto, quoted in "Notes on Genesis: 2009 Edition," Thomas L. Constable, www.soniclight.com/constable/notes/pdf/genesis.pdf.

6. William D. Mounce, *Mounce's Complete Expository Dictionary of Old and New Testament Words* (Grand Rapids, MI: Zondervan Publishing House, 2006), 332.

7. Genesis 2:18,20.

8. Exodus 18:4; Deuteronomy 33:7,26,29; Psalm 20:2; 33:20; 70:5; 89:19; 115:9,10,11; 121:1,2; 124:8; 146:5; Hosea 13:9.

9. Isaiah 30:5; Ezekiel 12:14; Daniel 11:34.

10. Mounce, *Mounce's Complete Expository Dictionary of Old and New Testament Words*, 332.

11. James, *When Life and Beliefs Collide*, 181.

12. Victor P. Hamilton, *The Book of Genesis, Chapters 1-17*, The International Commentary on the Old Testament, R.K. Harrison, ed. (Grand Rapids, MI: Eerdmans, 1990), 175.

13. James, *When Life and Beliefs Collide*, 185.

14. In several Bible passages, God told men to listen to women. He told Abraham, "Listen to whatever Sarah tells you" (Genesis 21:12). King Josiah consulted the prophetess Huldah (2 Chronicles 34:22). Priscilla taught the evangelist, Apollos (Acts 18:26).

15. Plato, *Timaeus*, trans. H.D.P. Lee (Baltimore, MD: Penguin, 1965), 42A-C, 90C, 91A.

16. John Temple Bristow, *What Paul Really Said About Women* (San Francisco, CA: HarperSanFrancisco, 1988), 5.

17. Dickason, "Anatomy and Destiny: The Role of Biology in Plato's Views of Women."

18. Plato, *Timaeus* in *Plato, Volume V.1: Timaeus, Critias, Cleitophon, Menexenus, Epistles*, trans. R.G. Gury (Cambridge, MA: Loeb Classical Library, Harvard University Press, 1941), 91a-d.

19. Aristotle, *Politics*, trans. Oxford University, *The Basic Works of Aristotle*, Richard McKeon, editor (New York, NY: Random House, 1941), 1.1234B.

20. Demosthenes, Adv. Neaeram, 122. Quotation by Marcus Barth, *The Anchor Bible* (New York, NY: Doubleday, 1979), vol. 34A, 655.

21. Stephen Jay Gould, *Hen's Teeth and Horse's Toes* (New York, NY: Norton, 1984), 244.

22. Eva Cantarella, *Pandora's Daughters: The Role and Status of Women in Greek and Roman Antiquity*, trans. Maureen B. Fant (Baltimore, MD: Johns Hopkins University Press, 1981), 143.

23. Cato the Elder, on the Dowry, quoted in Aulus Gellius, *Attic Nights*, 10.23.

24. Bristow, *What Paul Really Said About Women*, 12.

25. Loren Cunningham and David Joel Hamilton, *Why Not Women?* (Seattle, WA: YWAM Publishing, 2000), 108.

26. Leonard Swidler, *Biblical Affirmations of Woman* (Philadelphia, PA: Westminster John Knox Press, 1979), 163.

27. William Barclay, *Daily Study Bible*, 2nd ed. (Edinburgh: St. Andrews Press, 1958), vol.2, 142-3.

28. Aida Dina Besançon Spencer, *Beyond the Curse* (Nashville, TN: Thomas Nelson, 1985), 56.

29. Ross Saunders, *Outrageous Women, Outrageous God* (Alexandria, New South Wales, Australia: E.J. Dwyer, 1996), 18.

30. Gilbert Bilezikian, *Beyond Sex Roles* (Grand Rapids, MI: Baker Publishing Group, 1985), 60.

31. J.I. Packer, *Knowing God* (Chicago, IL: InterVarsity Press, 1973), 14-15.

32. John 7:16; 8:28; 12:49.

33. John 5:19,30; John 6:28,38.

34. Colossians 1:15.

35. Hebrews 1:3.

Chapter 2—Just an Ordinary Girl

1. W.E. Vine, Merrill F. Unger, and William White Jr., *Vine's Complete Expository Dictionary of Old and New Testament Words* (Nashville, TN: Thomas Nelson Publishers, 1985), 73.

2. Carolyn Custis James, *Lost Women of the Bible* (Grand Rapids, MI: Zondervan Publishing, 2005), 180.

Chapter 3—The Fearless Follower

1. Mary R. Thompson, *Mary of Magdala: Apostle and Leader* (New York, NY: Paulist, 1995), 47.

2. "Mary Magdalene: The Hidden Apostle," Biography, prod. Bram Roos, A&E Television Networks, 2000, videocassette, as quoted by Liz Curtis Higgs in *Mad Mary* (Colorado Springs, CO: WaterBrook, 2001), 143.

3. Higgs, *Mad Mary*, 142.

4. Neal W. May, *Israel: A Biblical Tour of the Holy Land* (Tulsa, OK: Albury, 2000), 244.

5. Higgs, *Mad Mary*, 150.

6. Susan Haskins, *Mary Magdalene: Myth and Metaphor* (New York, NY: Harcourt Brace & Co., 1993), 63.

7. Frank E. Gaebelein, ed., *The Expositor's Bible Commentary*, vol. 8 (Grand Rapids, MI: Zondervan, 1992), 584.

8. Matthew Henry, *Matthew Henry's Commentary of the Whole Bible*, vol. 5 (1706; reprint, Peabody, MA: Hendrickson, 1991), 672.

9. Higgs, *Mad Mary*, 233.

10. Gaebelein, ed., *The Expositor's Bible Commentary*, vol. 9, 192.

11. Higgs, *Mad Mary*, 251.

12. Ibid., 252.

13. James, *Lost Women of the Bible,* 187.

14. A. Kenneth Curtis and Daniel Graves, eds., *Great Women in Christian History* (Camp Hill, PA: WingSpread Publishers, 2004), 35-41.

15. Ralph D. Winter, as quoted in Cunningham and Hamilton, *Why Not Women?,* 26.

16. Melody and Keith Green, as quoted in Cunningham and Hamilton, *Why Not Women?,* 27.

17. Helen Kooiman Hosier, *100 Christian Women Who Changed the 20th Century* (Grand Rapids, MI: Fleming Revel, 2000), 255.

18. Joy Jacobs, *They Were Women Like Me* (Camp Hill, PA: Christian Publications, 1993), 144.

Chapter 4—The Chronically Ill Bold Believer

1. Erwin Lutzer and Rebecca Lutzer, *Jesus, Lover of a Woman's Soul* (Carol Stream, IL: Tyndale House Publishers, Inc., 2006), 86.

2. New English Bible (Oxford, England: Oxford University Press, 1961), note the end of the Gospel of John.

Chapter 5—The Ashamed Adulteress

1. Matthew 7:28-29; John 2:13-17; John 2:19.

2. John 4:4-42; John 4:43-54; John 5:1-9; John 6:1-13.

3. Nathaniel Hawthorne, *The Scarlet Letter,* as quoted in Liz Curtis Higgs, *Really Bad Girls of the Bible* (Colorado Springs, CO: Waterbrook, 2000), 79.

4. Herbert Lockyer, *All the Women of the Bible* (Grand Rapids, MI: Zondervan, 1967), 240.

5. David Thomas, *Gospel of John* (Grand Rapids, MI: Kregel Publications, 1980), 219.

6. Lutzer and Lutzer, *Jesus, Lover of a Woman's Soul,* 102.

Chapter 6—The Weary Woman at the Well

1. Linda H. Hollies, *Jesus and Those Bodacious Women* (Cleveland, OH: The Pilgrim Press, 2007), 84.

2. Liz Curtis Higgs, *Bad Girls of the Bible* (Colorado Springs, CO: Waterbrook, 1999), 91.

3. www.afb.org/MyLife/book.asp?ch=P1CH4.

4. John MacArthur, *The MacArthur Bible Commentary* (Nashville, TN: Thomas Nelson, 2005), 1364.

5. Peter Kreeft, *Three Philosophies of Life* (San Francisco, CA: Ignatius Press, 1989), 99.

6. C.S. Lewis, *The Silver Chair* (New York, NY: Macmillan Publishing Company, 1953), 15-17.

7. www.uni-ulm.de/LiLL/3.0/D/frauen/biografien/Jh19/boothen.html.

8. Vinson Synan, "Women in Ministry," *Ministries Today* (January/February, 1993), 46.

9. "The Preacher's Daughter," *Time* (May 1, 2000), 56-57.

10. Michael Richardson, *Amazing Faith: The Authorized Biography of Bill Bright* (Colorado Springs, CO: WaterBrook Press, 2000), 220.

11. Barbara Hudson Powers, *The Henrietta Mears Story* (Old Tappan, NJ: Fleming H. Revell Company, 1957), 7.

Chapter 7—The Winsome Worshipper

1. Matthew 7:1-3; Matthew 9:12-13; Matthew 9:2,6.
2. Luke 4:18-19.
3. Higgs, *Bad Girls of the Bible*, 229.
4. *NIV Archaeological Study Bible*, 1746.
5. A more complete telling of this story is found in Sharon Jaynes, *Becoming Spiritually Beautiful* (Eugene, OR: Harvest House Publishers, 2009), 187-89.

Chapter 8—The Daring Disciple

1. James B. Hurley, *Man and Woman in Biblical Perspective* (Grand Rapids, MI: Zondervan Publishing House, 1981), 72.
2. Josephus, *Against Apion*, 2.201.
3. Michael Griffiths, *The Example of Jesus* (Downers Grove, IL: InterVarsity Press), 132.
4. James, *When Life and Beliefs Collide*, 39-40.
5. Matthew 20:18-19.
6. B.F. Wescott, *Gospel According to St. John* (New York, NY: Doubleday, 1966), 178.
7. Ibid., 454.
8. James, *When Life and Beliefs Collide*, 167.
9. Ibid., 18.
10. Vinson Synan, "Women in Ministry," *Ministries Today* (January/February 1993), 46.

Chapter 9—The Stellar Student

1. James, *When Life and Beliefs Collide*, 114.
2. M.L. del Mastro, *All the Women of the Bible* (Edison, NJ: Castle Books, 2004), 270.
3. Ibid.

Chapter 10—The Bent but Brave

1. Psalm 3:3 KJV.
2. *NIV Archaeological Study Bible* (Grand Rapids, MI: Zondervan Publishing House, 2005), 1648.
3. Cunningham and Hamilton, *Why Not Women?*, 116.
4. Kenneth Barker, General Editor, *NIV Study Bible* (Grand Rapids, MI: Zondervan Publishing House, 1995), 1500-1501 (footnote on Mark 5:22).
5. Cunningham and Hamilton, *Why Not Women?*, 116.
6. Hollies, *Jesus and Those Bodacious Woman*, 44.

Chapter 12—The Gracious Giver

1. Alice Gray, "The Treasure," *Stories from the Heart—The Second Collection* (Sisters, OR: Multnomah Publishers, Inc., 1997), 147-48. Used by permission.

Chapter 13—God Calling Women Center Stage

1. Bilezikian, *Beyond Sex Roles*, 61.
2. Lutzer and Lutzer, *Jesus, Lover of a Woman's Soul*, xii.
3. Carolyn Custis James, *The Gospel of Ruth* (Grand Rapids, MI: Zondervan Publishing House, 2008), 66.

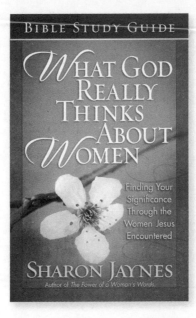

WHAT GOD REALLY THINKS ABOUT WOMEN
BIBLE STUDY GUIDE

For those ready to dig a little deeper into the thoughts God has about women, Sharon has written a companion Bible study guide to her book *What God Really Thinks About Women*. Let this insightful and inviting study draw you into a more confident relationship with your heavenly Father.

With her trademark biblical perspective, Sharon spends time with Jesus' mother, the woman at the well, Mary Magdalene, and others, and brings to life their encounters with the forgiveness, healing, and love of Jesus.

Great for group or personal exploration, this revealing study guide provides passage studies, reflective questions, and exciting discoveries about God's love for His daughters then and now.

Awaken to God's heart and hope for you as He lovingly exchanges heartache, hopelessness, doubt, or shame for the beauty of wholeness.

About the Author

Sharon Jaynes is an international inspirational speaker and Bible teacher for women's conferences and events. She is the author of several books, including *Becoming the Woman of His Dreams, The Power of a Woman's Words, Your Scars Are Beautiful to God, Becoming Spiritually Beautiful, "I'm Not Good Enough"...and Other Lies Women Tell Themselves,* and *Becoming a Woman Who Listens to God.* Her books have been translated into several foreign languages and impact women around the globe. Her passion is to encourage, equip, and empower women to walk in courage and confidence as they grasp their true identity as a child of God and a co-heir with Christ.

Sharon is a cofounder of Girlfriends in God, a conference and online ministry that crosses denominational, racial, and generational boundaries to unify the body of Christ. To learn more visit www.girlfriendsinGod.com.

Sharon and her husband, Steve, have one grown son, Steven. They call North Carolina home.

Sharon is always honored to hear from her readers. You can contact her directly at Sharon@sharonjaynes.com or at her mailing address:

Sharon Jaynes
PO Box 725
Matthews, NC 28106

To learn more about Sharon's books and speaking ministry or to inquire about having her speak at your next event, visit www.sharonjaynes.com.

Other Books
By Sharon Jaynes

YOUR SCARS ARE BEAUTIFUL TO GOD
Sharon shares with women how emotional scars can lead to healing and restoration. Encouraging chapters and inspirational stories reveal how you can give your past pains over to the One who turns hurt into hope and heartache into happiness.

BUILDING AN EFFECTIVE WOMEN'S MINISTRY
This unique yet practical how-to manual offers a wide range of help to women, from those just starting out to those who have a thriving ministry but could use a fresh idea or two. For groups large and small, this is a treasure trove of detailed information on how to serve and care for women.

BECOMING THE WOMAN OF HIS DREAMS
Sharon provides a thoughtful look at the wonderful, unique, and God-ordained role a woman has in her husband's life. If you would like a little "wow!" back in your relationship with the man you married, let seven simple secrets, biblical wisdom, and tender stories of both men and women inspire you to truly be the wife your husband longs for.

BECOMING A WOMAN WHO LISTENS TO GOD
"When I pour over the pages of Scripture," says Sharon, "I discover that some of God's most memorable messages were not delivered while men and women were away on a spiritual retreat, but right in the middle of the hustle and bustle of everyday life. He spoke to Moses while he was tending sheep, to Gideon while he was threshing wheat, to the woman at the well while she was drawing water for her housework. It is not a matter of does He speak, but will we listen." Discover with Sharon what it means to become a woman who listens to God.

HARVEST HOUSE
PUBLISHERS

"I'M NOT GOOD ENOUGH"...AND OTHER LIES WOMEN TELL THEMSELVES

Sharon looks at the common lies women tell themselves and shows them how they can replace those lies with Truth. Her book is a handy reference tool that will help women renew their minds and think God's thoughts rather than be swayed by the enemy's deceptions.

BECOMING SPIRITUALLY BEAUTIFUL

In *Becoming Spiritually Beautiful*, Sharon gently shares how becoming spiritually beautiful is something full of promise and possibilities. Spiritual beauty brings new beginnings, fresh faith, and the hope of a beauty unique in the universe.

EXTRAORDINARY MOMENTS WITH GOD

How do ordinary days become filled with extraordinary moments? When people listen to God's still small voice and see His fingerprints on the pages of their lives. These stories will enable readers to see how God is moving in the lives of fellow travelers and to recognize God's presence in their own lives.

THE POWER OF A WOMAN'S WORDS

The Power of a Woman's Words is for every woman who desires to use her words to build up rather than tear down, to encourage rather than discourage, to cheer rather than jeer. It is for all who desire to have more control over that mighty force called the tongue.

A WOMAN'S SECRET TO A BALANCED LIFE

Coauthored with Lysa TerKeurst, this essential book offers seven vital ways any Christian woman can prioritize her life more effectively.

HARVEST HOUSE
PUBLISHERS

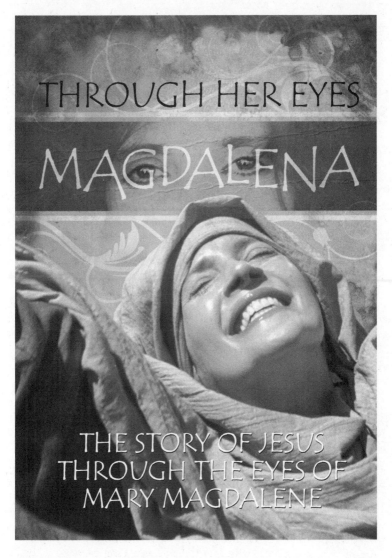

To watch a few of the women's stories you just read about, visit www.MagdalenaToday.com and order your copy of the DVD.

www.MagdalenaToday.com